# All [A]

# Your Journey to Becoming a Corporate Director

MW00954485

Olga V. Mack

# Table of Contents

Introduction   1

1. Understanding Boards   4

What does the board of directors do?   5

What are the time commitments of a board member?   10

How much does a board director get paid?   12

How do I assess my qualifications for board service?   15

What factors generally influence corporate board composition?   17

What is the audit committee and what qualifications do I need to serve on it?   19

What is a nomination committee and what qualifications do I need to serve on it?   22

What helps a board of directors be effective?   25

Are board placement services right for me?   28

What is the ideal size of a nonprofit board of directors?   33

2. Types of Boards   36

What type of boards exist?   37

What is a startup and what is a startup board?   41

How do I join a startup board of directors or advisory board?   43

What is a startup advisory board and what factors should I consider before joining a startup advisory board?   46

How are startup board of directors members compensated?   48

What is a family business and what kind of board
opportunities does a family business have?     50

What can I bring to a family business board as an
independent director?     52

What are advisory boards and why should I serve on
them?     57

What's the difference between a board of directors and an
advisory board?     61

3. Why serve?     64

Why should I serve on a corporate board of directors?     65

What makes board service a great leadership
opportunity?     68

Cultural awareness: what is it, why is it important, and how
can I leverage it?     72

What are the major questions to ask myself before joining a
board of directors?     75

What are the risks that come with serving on a corporate
board of directors?     78

4. How to get on a corporate board     82

What should I consider before deciding to serve on a
corporate board as a director?     83

How can I choose the right board for me?     86

How do I get a position on a corporate board of directors? 90

What can I do now to become ready to serve on a corporate
board?     93

What are the characteristics and attributes of an ideal board
member?     97

How can I develop key skills to serve as a corporate board member? 101

How can I identify and address the skills I am missing to serve on a corporate board of directors? 105

Generally, what factors are considered in corporate board of directors selection? 108

How can I build great relationships that can lead to a corporate board of directors seat? 109

5. Practical steps to get on a corporate board 113

How can I elevate my profile to get a board seat? 114

How can I effectively use LinkedIn? 119

How can I position my skills, expertise, experience, and knowledge? 122

Why is a corporate board biography important, and how can I write one effectively? 127

How can I choose a board opportunity that will boost my career? 130

How can I network to get on a corporate board of directors? 133

What is P&L and why should a corporate board member master it? How can I leverage my P&L experience? 135

6. Who can join a corporate board? 137

What is angel investing? How can I leverage angel investing to join a corporate board of directors? 138

What experiences can lawyers bring to a corporate board of directors? What qualities should they emphasize? 140

Do academics qualify to serve on corporate boards of directors? What qualities should they emphasize?    144

Do entrepreneurs qualify to serve on a corporate board of directors? What qualities should they emphasize?    146

Do professionals with financial backgrounds qualify to serve on a corporate board of directors? What qualities should they emphasize?    148

Do private equity professionals qualify to serve on a corporate board of directors? What qualities should they emphasize?    151

Do engineers and other technical professionals qualify to serve on a corporate board of directors? What qualities should they emphasize?    153

When am I too old to serve on a corporate board?    156

Why should I start pursuing my corporate director career when I am young?    158

7. Due diligence    163

What are the right ways to research target companies for a corporate director position?    164

What should I look for during due diligence on a corporate board?    167

How can I conduct due diligence on a startup before joining its board?    169

What are the red flags to look out for when searching for a corporate board of directors position?    172

8. Interviewing    175

How can I leave a good first impression as a prospective board member?    176

What should I expect at a corporate board of directors interview? 178

What should I do before my corporate board of directors interview? 180

What should I do during the corporate board of directors interview? 182

What should I look for when I interview for a corporate board position? 186

What should I avoid at the corporate board of directors interview? 188

What should I do after my corporate board of directors interview? 191

Conclusion 193

Appendix A 194

Appendix B 207

Appendix C 210

Appendix D 215

Appendix E 253

About the Author 258

# Introduction

Over a year ago, I started the Women Serve on Boards movement. Our goal was simple: pressure the remaining Fortune 500 companies with all-male boards to discover their first woman directors. Two petitions, a few letters, and countless social media posts later, we convinced some Fortune 500 companies to hire their first women for their boards of directors.

In a process of advocating for this cause, I was thrilled to learn that many professionals – men and women – are pursuing or at least considering board service. I also realized that the process of becoming a director seems mysterious to many professionals. Many imagine that an invisible hand takes a few select professionals and gives them a corporate board seat.

This, of course, is a myth. The reality is much more intentional than magical.

I have spoken with and interviewed many directors, chairmen, CEOs, recruiters, and other professionals who assist boards. They all reveal that becoming a corporate director is a journey that takes one to five years. It involves a lot of educating, networking, and strategic positioning.

In other words, just like everything worth pursuing, it mostly involves a lot of hard work! Yes, there are occasional glimpses of luck. But there are definitely no "magical" moments, invisible hands, or other miracles.

Throughout my advocacy work, many professionals (both supporters and strangers) have approached me with practical questions about board service. Their questions range from "Why pursue board service?" to "How can I join a board?"

At first the process of answering questions was exciting, especially because it allowed me to expand my professional network. Over time, however, I found myself answering the same questions many times over.

I realized that no matter how much I'd like to, I can't have lunch, coffee, or even a phone call with everyone who wants to learn more about boards. So, I've written down all the questions that I have been repeatedly answering, and compiled the answers into this book. This way I can help more professionals.

This book is a beginners' guide for those who are considering becoming a director. It answers basic questions and shares actionable strategies. This book is for professionals at all stages in their careers. It is useful to young professionals, as it suggests what jobs and assignments they need to seek if they may want to pursue board service in the future. It is also useful to professionals who are contemplating becoming a director in the near future or who have just started their board journeys.

Of course, there are more comprehensive guides and consultants who can hold your hand through your director journey. Depending on your goals and resources, you may consider using these resources as well. I have listed some of them in Appendix C.

This book is aimed to be a short and easy read that answers many initial questions, demystifies the process, and shares actionable strategies that you can implement today. It can be read in any order.

My hope is that after reading this book, any professional will be convinced that corporate board service is within their reach. It is not for the select, highly connected, famous, and wealthy few. And, it certainly doesn't require any "magic."

Clear intention, coherent strategy, time investment, and flawless execution are all you need to eventually make your director dream a reality.

Have a great corporate director journey, enjoy the ride, and – perhaps most importantly – share your stories, strategies, templates, worksheets, and tips with me at http://olgamack.com/contact/. I may incorporate them in the next edition of this book.

Let's learn and celebrate together!

# 1. Understanding Boards

Boards are an incredibly complex facet of corporate culture. Before pursuing board service, it can be helpful to have a foundational understanding of boards. This includes time commitments, compensation, composition, and special committees. This section describes all of the above, as well as other board fundamentals.

# What does the board of directors do?

The board of directors is composed of the key people who make decisions about important issues, hire the CEO, and perform a number of other roles and responsibilities. They are the governing body of a company. These decision makers carry almost all the power to run a company.

For example, hiring a CEO, making any major acquisition, selling the company, and numerous other key events all require board approval. Because the board determines the overall strategy of the company, they must be engaged, diligent, responsible, and have a high degree of integrity.

**Here are some of the responsibilities of the board of directors:**

**Recruiting, retaining, supervising, compensating, and evaluating the CEO.** This is the most prominent function of a board of directors. This is the main reason that only a skilled, experienced, and capable candidate gets the chance to join a board.

**Determining the strategic plans of a company.** This includes taking care of the company's financial stability, selecting its target market, and designing the present and future plans of the company.

**Guiding and overseeing the company in the right direction.** The board is responsible for creating the organization's vision and goals.

**Controlling and monitoring various functions of the board.** For example, the board is responsible for monitoring the auditing process. The board hires auditors and related staff.

**Maximizing long-term shareholder returns and protecting the company's assets and investments.** This responsibility applies to boards of public companies.

**Supervising a search for the right investors.** The board makes major advance decisions for the company.

**Assisting the owner, the CEO, and other members of the leadership team.** Board members assist with making key decisions, facilitating introductions, oversight, and inquiries.

Of course, the prime responsibility of every Board Member is to help in the effective functioning of the organization while ensuring no interruptions in the output.

Here are some of the core activities of a board member:

## Guide and interact with the CEO

The core function of a board member is to cooperate with the CEO of the organization. Board members select the CEO and, if some outstanding conditions prevail, the board members also have the power to remove the CEO. The board members evaluate the work of the CEO while monitoring his or her decisions and performance toward the organization. They encourage the CEO to handle situations effectively, aiding him or her to take better decisions.

## Consider strategies

Board members must constantly keep raising questions about the strategies that the organization follows for each project, big and small. The purpose of this is to avoid any negative after-effects of a strategy by discussing its planning and working on its implementation. Board members review these strategies, focusing on their advantages and disadvantages and predicting any proportion of loss or profit that can be received.

This discussion about strategies occurs majorly among the board members, the CEO and senior officers.

## Monitor the functioning of management

Board members play an important role in the organization by monitoring the performance of the management. They review each and every task or project taken up by management and keenly observe the activities and the policies followed.

This role looks different in profit-bearing organizations, compared to in nonprofit organizations. It is not a compact job to operate in a profit-bearing organization. But these organizations certainly fulfil their established goals through the means of their policies.

On the other hand, nonprofit organizations have a completely difficult scenario. Board members often face difficulty, as it is impossible to indicate whether the organization has met its goals in the past few years or not.

## Safeguard the values of the organization

The board members also the operating method of the organization in check. They ensure that the organization should always progress in the right way – responsibly and effectively.

The board members also ensure that all the activities that are taking place in the organization are conducted with ethical and legal responsibilities in mind. Board members also keep an eye on expenses and the output that is produced in return.

# What are the time commitments of a board member?

Serving on a board of directors offers many opportunities and responsibilities. However, board members must invest significant time to fulfill their responsibilities for the company. They must prepare for and attend board meetings, provide guidance, understand and analyze financial strategy, serve on committees, and fulfill numerous other obligations.

The role of the board of directors is increasingly more complex and often time-consuming. Most boards meet at least four times in a year. In some companies, the board meets more often. The board may also meet more often if certain circumstances, such as a merger or acquisition, occur. Most board members spend more than 40 hours every year preparing for board meetings, and at least 30 hours every year traveling for board-related activities. Many of them also spend at least 30 hours every year serving various committees of the board.

**Key time commitments include:**

Considering strategies for the development of business

Keeping an eye on industry trends, the development of the business, and any applicable laws

Providing guidance to the chairperson, company leadership, and the management team

Meeting with the professional and financial advisors of the company

Serving on board committees

Traveling for formal and informal events

There are numerous other responsibilities a board member may have, which can vary based on the organization and board type. If you are joining a board it is important to discuss the time commitments and expectations first. You have to make it sure that you are ready to meet the expectations and obligations that may come with your appointment.

# How much does a board director get paid?

The compensation of the board of directors varies across experiences, sectors, and geographies. They also vary across different boards – the advisory board, private board, public boards, nonprofit board, startup boards, family boards, and others.

## Public boards

On public boards, board member compensation is generally divided between stock and cash. Most of the board members receive a certain amount of shares from the stock of the company. The total compensation for each individual member depends on different factors, such as how long they have been involved with the company, their specific skills or knowledge, whether they have a high public profile, and many other factors. Board members who are greatly sought after can obtain a substantial total compensation.

By the Boston Globe's calculations, the median pay in 2014 for a board seat at a micro-cap company (one with less than $500 million in revenues) was $105,583. Pay increases with company size, ranging up to $258,000 for board members of the 200 largest U.S. corporations (those with more than $10 billion in revenues).

## Private boards

While there is a lot of variance in compensation for private boards, a well-established private board generally offers higher compensation to its prospective board members. It is not unusual for a medium-sized private company to offer prospective board members somewhere between $15,000 to $40,000 per year. Some private companies offer compensation similar to that offered by micro-cap public companies, especially if they have $200 to $500 million in revenue. This comes to around $100,000.

## Advisory boards

Compensation for advisory board members varies dramatically. It is not unusual for an advisory board member to not to be compensated or to receive only an equity grant, especially at startups. Some companies pay between $250 to $1,500 for each meeting attended, give stock in the company, or pay members to participate in the annual strategic session for about $5,000. But this is not true for all startups. Therefore, before joining an advisory board it is very important to have a very honest discussion about your time commitments and expected compensation.

## Nonprofit boards

Serving on a nonprofit board is often a volunteer activity. Usually, nonprofit boards do not compensate their directors. Only a small number of nonprofit organizations pay their members. Therefore, before joining a nonprofit board, consider having a very honest discussion about your time commitments and obligations.

# How do I assess my qualifications for board service?

Here are some questions that you need to ask yourself in other to check if you are qualified for board service.

## Am I passionate about this company?

This is very important! If the answer is no, you probably don't need to ask any more questions. You need to ask yourself whether you are passionate about helping the company get to its desired heights. Are you interested in the vision and mission of the company?

## Am I knowledgeable enough?

As a potential board member, you must be knowledgeable in various aspects of your discipline, industry, and the company. This doesn't mean that board members aren't prone to mistakes or that they don't have flaws. But you a certain level of knowledge is required to be a qualified candidate.

## Am I yearning to learn?

Serving on a board means you must be open-minded, ask good questions, know how to work with experts, and stay on top of the industry. This means that you must have the mindset to learn new concepts and ideas that can make you better as an individual.

## How do I relate with others?

Don't forget that a board comprises of more than one person. Each member of a board has valuable knowledge, life experiences, and industry expertise. The major question is whether you can interact very well with them without any form of negativity surfacing after a while. There will be times when you are likely to experience disagreements, whether tactical or philosophical ones. How do you handle such situations? How would you influence the outcome you want to see?

## Can I serve?

Being a board member places you in a position where you are serving the company. After all, on a public company board and on many private company boards your goal is to maximize long-term return for the company's shareholders. You need to know whether you can withstand the challenges of the role and serve the company well. This involves time commitment, willingness to learn, and an uncompromising dedication to realizing the company's goals.

The *Board Profile and Competency Matrix* worksheet in Appendix B can help you to identify the experience, knowledge, and skills that you can leverage for board service.

# What factors generally influence corporate board composition?

Corporate board composition is typically closely related to issues of board independence and the various experiences of autonomous outside directors. Companies must balance these competing interests when they consider the composition of their corporate boards:

**Status quo vs. new perspective**

Against the foundation of recent historic worldwide financial downturns, companies often want to enlist directors with new perspectives who also possess experience and skills appropriate to the current difficulties. There is also a developing appreciation for diverse boards, which are more likely to pose essential inquiries instead of surrendering to "general thinking." However, boards also need to protect and use their current institutional information and connections. They also need to have a long-term vision and create sense of stability for all major stakeholders such as employees, investors, leadership, management, and regulators.

## Structure vs. diversity

Corporate boards of directors, especially at more established organizations, have frequently set a standard for choosing directors who can fit effortlessly into existing board culture and will work well with existing members of the board and leadership. Therefore, CEOs, executives, and selection committees often rely on their professional or social networks for recruiting directors. This tendency, of course, strengthens board composition homogeneity. However, homogeneous boards are weak and insufficient to meet the needs and wants of diverse clients, partners, employees, suppliers, investors, and other key stakeholders.

## Granular proficiency vs. long-term oversight

Corporate boards have put less emphasis on recruiting corporate directors with specific capabilities related to the company or industry. Generally speaking, a corporate board of directors oversees its company's direction to maximize the company's long-term returns to its shareholders. They generally do not manage day-to-day operations. However, it can be an asset for a corporate director to understand the company, its industry, and its historic evolution. In fact, many suggest that it is paramount in the success of a corporate director.

# What is the audit committee and what qualifications do I need to serve on it?

## Audit committee

In the international market, the audit committee is an operating committee of the board of directors that is responsible for supervising the financial reporting and disclosure process of the respective company or organization. The committee members are chosen from the board of directors, by the chairperson of the organization. It is one of the most important committees and is required for many companies.

## Types

There are two types of audit committees: external audit committees and the other one is internal audit committees.

## Role of the audit committee

All United States publicly-traded companies must maintain a qualified audit committee in order to be listed on a stock exchange. The necessity of the audit committee can fluctuate from country to country depending on the law.

There are many responsibilities of the audit committee, including:

Supervising financial reports

Monitoring the choice of accounting policies

Discussing risk management policies

Overseeing the performance of the internal audit committee

Supervising ethics

Monitoring the internal control process

Overseeing the external auditors

These responsibilities of the audit committee are assigned by committee charter. There are often six members of the audit committee. Among other things, The New York Stock Exchange (NYSE) and the Nasdaq Stock Market (NASDAQ) require that each company appoint at least three directors, all of whom must be independent, to an audit committee.

**Essential qualifications**

At a minimum, each member of the committee has to be financially literate. Accounting or financial management experience is important, if not required. One member of the committee has to be an "audit committee financial expert," as required by the U.S. Securities and Exchange Commission (SEC). The audit committee members and the chairperson have to be nominated and elected by the board itself.

## Primary purpose

The primary purpose of the audit committee is to check on financial reports. To do so, they hold regularly scheduled meetings and maintain a connection between the board of directors, the financial management of the organization, internal auditors, and independent auditors.

While the audit committee has various responsibilities and powers, it is not the duty of the audit committee to plan or generate financial statements. This is the responsibility of the management team and the independent auditors.

# What is a nomination committee and what qualifications do I need to serve on it?

### What is a nomination committee?

A nomination committee is a group of corporate directors who have the power and responsibility to ensure that the board of directors is properly evaluated. It may also review and change corporate governance policies.

It is the duty of the nomination committee to ensure that the skills and characteristics of potential board members have been properly evaluated or investigated. In other words, a nomination committee acts as a link between potential board members and the board itself.

The nomination committee is often composed of five board members, who are often expected to serve for about two years. The committee is often comprised of the chairman of the board, the deputy chairman, and the chief executive officer.

# Required qualifications of nomination committee members

Below are some of the qualifications that are required for a member of the board to serve on a nomination committee in most companies.

## Confidentiality

As a member of the nomination committee, you are not expected to disclose the nomination committee's discussions non-nomination committee members. If you join the nomination committee you need to be comfortable with being even more discreet than other board members.

## Sound judgement

As a member of the nomination committee, you must understand how to clearly interpret issues that relate to the board of directors, company governance, and the company's long-term strategic vision. This implies that you must know what is expected of every board member at different periods of time and what each member brings to the table. Such judgements must not only be unbiased but must also reflect the aims and objectives of the company.

## Integrity

As a member of the nomination committee, will be trusted to carry out duties with the utmost integrity.

This means that members of the nomination committee are expected to sustain the values of the company through a high level of integrity that will reflect whenever they are carrying out their duties. For instance, potential nominees of the committee are expected to be given purely objective considerations that take the company's strategic long-term goals and vision into account.

**Diversity of thought and knowledge**

As a member of a nomination committee, you must possess diverse experiences and sound knowledge about various fields. This will help you clearly and accurately evaluate candidates from various fields and backgrounds.

# What helps a board of directors be effective?

A great board is always very diverse in perspectives, background, thought, and representation. After all, the board of directors must make important decisions for the company. For example, the board of directors may fire or hire a CEO or other members of the executive staff. The corporate board of directors is ultimately accountable to the shareholders of the company.

While good governance is necessary for a functioning board of directors, these practices can also help boards be more effective:

**Regular attendance at corporate board meetings**

Arranging and attending regular meetings is the hallmark of a careful and responsible director. *All* of the members must prioritize regularly attending meetings. Studies have demonstrated that regular attendance can truly impact the success of a company and its board of directors. Attending board meetings is a way to make important decisions, bond, and share experience, knowledge, skills, and strategies.

**Diversity of skills and experiences**

To run a board successfully, each corporate director must bring strategic and valuable experiences, insights, knowledge, and expertise. Their complementary skills and attributes can benefit the company and may even increase the company's revenue. It is important to have board members who are well qualified, skilled, smart, and collaborative.

## Diversity of thought

On average, diverse corporate boards of directors make better decisions than homogeneous corporate boards of directors. Therefore, in addition to diversity of skills and experiences, it is a good idea to make sure that a board of directors also exhibits diversity in other categories such as gender, age, race, sexual orientation, geography, national origin, and thought.

## Maintaining a clear and distinct role

One of the biggest wellsprings of contention happens when the members of the corporate board endeavor to overstep their roles from oversight to management. Corporate boards of directors are occasionally confused about their roles. It is critical for the board of directors to go through important issues and oversee without managing.

## Moral ownership

The corporate board of directors members are the moral owners of the company. It is important that they are people of high integrity with long records of flawless judgment. This way their actions and words can inspire a company and its leadership to stay on course.

## Implementing key policies

Among the greatest difficulties for organizations is having a clearly articulated reason or purpose for existing. Organizations can frequently lose all sense of direction in hectic administrations. Comprehending where the company is endeavoring to go or whether it has been effective should be the primary focus of boards in a governing role.

## Well-planned board of directors and committee meetings

It is critical for a successful board of directors to have a general meeting plan that spans the entire year, with a set agenda before each meeting. This way, the directors will meet regularly to discuss issues in a timely manner and make sure that their meetings are productive.

## Self-improvement responsibility

Each board of directors is responsible for its own execution and adequacy. Therefore, it should regularly inquire about the skills and experiences each director is bringing, the gaps that need to be filled, and the time frame for filling any gaps.

# Are board placement services right for me?

The recent hype about board service, especially for women and diverse candidates, is real. It seems like everyone is getting on board — or at least trying to. The increased interest in board service has led to a proliferation of board placement and board readiness services. These services offer appealing packages, intended to help potential board members become desirable candidates and find the positions of their dreams. Many seem like the "magic ticket" to a professional's first board position.

As an **outspoken advocate** for diverse boards, I get many questions about these services. Are they useful? How much do they cost? How should a hopeful board candidate choose from the many options? As much as I like to advise and encourage potential board candidates, I can never really answer these questions. They're just too subjective! Choosing a board placement or board readiness service is like choosing a car: the right one depends completely on you, your goals, and your preferences. It isn't an easy process, but by asking the right questions, you can get a feel for whether a specific placement or readiness service is right for you.

Not sure where to start? Here's a list of questions to ask any board placement or board readiness services:

## Geographic concerns

Where are the services offered? Where are the candidates placed? Does the service offer board placement or readiness services locally, nationally, and internationally? At a minimum, you want to make sure that the board placement or board readiness service meets at least some of your geographic needs and aspirations.

## Industry and network fit

Does the service offer boards from organizations in a wide variety of interest areas to address your goals? Does the service have connections in your industry? Does it place people in public, private, startup, or nonprofit boards that you are interested in? Does it have connections and trusted relationships with the executives, decision-makers, and influencers? It is important to ensure that the service's expertise, core competency, and network are of use to you.

## Track record of success

Does the service track its success metrics? How often does it place candidates? How frequently do the candidates it places work long term? Do its candidates tend to stay on boards where they are placed for at least three years? Does it publish its rates online? If not, why not? Does the service track how its candidates have performed once recruited for a board? Does the service provide a relatively comprehensive list of companies it has helped? How long has the service been in existence?

## Process logistics

If a service considers itself a board matching service, how many board positions does it offer each month or year? How many organizations does it serve regularly? Does it let you interview with more than one board opening at a time? It is also important to understand what, exactly, you are signing up for. How exactly does the algorithm or process work? How involved is the service, beyond simply identifying candidates? Is there someone at the service who will personally understand the company, their needs, and their experiences and then match you with the right board opportunity? Or, will you be invited to a board fair, or provided with a list or search engine to peruse board opportunities on your own? How does the service ensure quality control for matches? Finally, what are the credentials of the individuals who will be performing your search?

## Money matters

Who will pay for placing you, how much, and when? Will the company pay? Are you expected to pay? Is the payment tied to reaching any milestones? Are there different packages for different candidates or companies?

## Included and additional services

Does the service provide any other assistance, such as writing your board biography? Does it provide basic director training or interview coaching? Does it share research about the company, its executives, and its board members? Does the service stay involved throughout the matching process to answer questions and keep the interview process on track? What other value besides matching does the service provide? Is board matching the primary product this service offers, or do they offer other services such as executive placement, training, or coaching?

## Good to know

You may also want to understand whether the board specializes in certain demographics such as hiring initiatives for women, placing diverse candidates, or locating first-time board candidates. You may also need to know whether the service will allow you to work with other board placement or board readiness services simultaneously.

This list may seem overwhelming, but because board service is such an important career step, every question is important. After all, you wouldn't purchase a car without making sure all your bases were covered. Similarly, when choosing the right vehicle for this exciting career move, you need to shop smart and stay proactive to separate out the lemons.

Appendix C provides a list of *Board Search Resources*, which includes board placement services.

# What is the ideal size of a nonprofit board of directors?

The ideal size of a nonprofit board of directors varies on three major things:

The size the organization's budget, constituency, and staff

The nature of the company's constituency and mission

The expanded role of the board, defined by laws

**The importance of board sizes:**

Nonprofit boards rarely exceed 21 members. However, sometimes a good board for a nonprofit is smaller. A different or separate trustee board or advisory board may serve your purposes better. A board with a larger number of members may lose its effectiveness and efficiency.

This type of board may combine with smaller executive committees to conduct the ongoing business of the board on a regular basis. This program may ultimately serve the organization better if it recruits prominent members that can give the board a local presence and provide the local constituency with an active voice.

On the other hand, a board should never be less than 5 diverse members. Small boards may face more difficulty in representing their constituencies and have more potential for internal interest conflicts.

There are more exceptions too. Some organizations need larger boards because their support relies on the donor and public relationship. Some other agencies like social or the human service providers, like to have smaller boards because they have limited funding sources and limited sources, and must create the board with their major grant sources.

The size of a board depends majorly on the organization's expectations. The board of a professional association or an advocacy organization with a large, diverse, geographically isolated constituency may feel more connected with the relevant organization. These organizations may have legitimate reasons to have larger boards.

A policy board of a renowned organization may safely increase in size because it has an executive director who understands the relations of the board.

A mid-size board must often consider policy. This kind of board may utilize considerable leadership and time.

A board that provides professional level support through accounting, legal, and program expertise is typically smaller than others. It may have a substantial executive director to interact with the existing board members.

The ideal nonprofit board tends to vary between 7 and 15 members. Fewer (five or fewer) board members may not fulfill all the necessary tasks of the board. The board size depends majorly on the tasks that a board should accomplish. If the members come from different fields and have different skills, they can enrich the nonprofit board most effectively.

# 2. Types of Boards

When we discuss boards, we usually refer to corporate boards of directors for large public companies. But there are many other types of boards, such as startup boards and advisory boards. Serving on these boards can be valuable intrinsically or as a launching point to leverage into a position on a public company's board of directors. This section describes the various types of boards and the opportunities they present.

# What type of boards exist?

As you know, corporate boards are important because they are responsible for effectively serving their organizations. There are generally four broad types of boards. Each has their own unique responsibilities, major roles, and compositions.

All types of boards need strong leadership and operational powers regardless of purpose and size. Every board needs a complete delineation of expectations and responsibilities. They must also present a clear framework to support the organization to the best of their capabilities, including interacting with stakeholders and other company leadership. Their job is to do the best things for the organization, even beyond the walls of the board room.

Here are the four broad types of boards:

**Nonprofit boards**

Nonprofit boards serve a 501(c)(3) tax-exempt organization. Directors on these boards make a commitment to a cause that that they are passionate about. Board service on nonprofit boards often involves volunteering, fundraising, and/or philanthropic donation.

The primary reason to serve on nonprofit board should be an interest in the nonprofit's mission and impact. Serving on a nonprofit board is in itself a satisfying experience when your interests are aligned with the mission of the nonprofit organization. Depending on who else is serving, how structured and organized the board is, and what your specific role is, nonprofit board service may be an opportunity to learn and network while working hard for a cause you believe in. Depending on the nonprofit, prior board experience may not be required.

These opportunities are almost never paid but can be well worth it in terms of fulfilment and experience. Consider being clear about your responsibilities and expectations to make sure there are no surprises. Also, consider attending a few meetings to determine whether you really connect with the board's mission, structure, and people.

**Advisory boards a.k.a. councils**

Advisory boards exist to offer fine expertise and excellence to other boards or executives such as the CEO. Advisory boards also complement other functional areas of the organization, such as the management team or task forces. For any startup venture, advisory boards should be highly prioritized. One can set up an advisory board as part of the initial planning stage, but it will often turn out to be the pioneer for your organization. A well-managed and well-structured advisory board can enhance the bandwidth and ensure the right outcome for a non-profit organization.

These are usually non-governing boards with no fiduciary duty. Because of this, some don't believe that advisory boards should be called boards. Even if you prefer to call them "councils" instead of boards, they still merit consideration. Advisory boards often offer valuable professional opportunities and are a great way to start your board journey.

They provide a good first introduction to corporate board service. If you join one, consider being clear about expectations and what you will be able to contribute.

**Private corporate boards**

The working zone of the private board is vast. Private company boards serve not only small businesses, but also companies of all sizes – some quite large. These opportunities include large multinational private companies, co-ops, venture-backed startups, family businesses, and numerous others. They exist in many industries and geographies. It is worth exploring the richness and wealth of your options when it comes to private corporate boards. Generally speaking, private boards don't have as many legal and regulatory requirements as do public corporate boards. Therefore, private boards are often great springboards for corporate board service. However, your experiences will widely vary across companies, industries, and geographies.

## Public corporate boards

Public corporate boards are regulated and very structured. It is a serious, time-consuming role, though it may be well-compensated. As a public company director you must allocate time attend the meetings, prepare for meetings, serve on committees, and fulfill other responsibilities, especially in the time of crisis. Public corporate board positons take time to obtain as they are very selective and exclusive.

# What is a startup and what is a startup board?

A startup is a new business that is still being built. For new entrepreneurs, starting their own company is a huge undertaking. Most of them think that a startup board is not of importance, at least for the ground-breaking process. Over time, many startups that survive the first few years may re-think this position as they educate themselves about their industry, their business, and the value board members bring.

**The need for a startup board**

For every company, a board may be very important, if not necessary. When an entrepreneur is building her empire, she will assess her business, its needs, and the value she hopes the prospective board members board bring. The truth may be that startup businesses can be successful with or without a startup board. However, often the need for a board arises if there is an investor who demands that a board be formed. A board may also become necessary if an entrepreneur wants to address certain needs of her company.

**Startup board composition**

The people an entrepreneur chooses for her board are critical to her business' performance. As time progresses, she may need to involve more people with certain expertise, knowledge, or experience. Executives, senior management officers, former regulators, and industry leaders are among the people who may be included on a startup's board of directors. They may become key decision makers and even be hands-on involved in a startup.

**The role of the startup board**

Because there may not be a lot of information available about a startup, completing your due diligence on a company and its founder is especially important. Every startup board or advisory board member should work well together and have a shared understanding of the company, its founders, its goals, it investors, and its numerous other stakeholders.

# How do I join a startup board of directors or advisory board?

Any intentional board search starts with self-reflection. Ask yourself if you are ready to join the board, how much time you can invest in board service, and what you actually expect from the company that you are going to join. You also need to determine what your specific target audience is, as well as a process to leverage your network.

It is also very important to honestly consider the following issues:

**Understand the time commitment**

To join a board and to serve it successfully you need hands-on experience and a well-built network. Securing these is, of course, a time-consuming matter. If you are on one of the board's special committees you must also dedicate time to solving any unique problems that arise. Before joining a board, be sure about the time that you can give to your job and your organization to make it successful.

**Clearly articulate your value proposition to the board**

You will have a huge responsibility as a startup board member. The board will expect several commitments from you, including financial investments, philosophical boundaries, and much more. Only you can articulate what you actually offer, and only you can understand your true capacity. Ask yourself: In light of your education, experience, and expertise, what value do you bring to the companies you would like to serve? Also make sure you know the unique angle you want to bring to the board, such as a fresh industry perspective or a perfected, expert financial strategy.

**Craft your target market**

Determine your target market and know everything about it. Research will uncover the essentials, such as location, size and industry. What companies are you a particularly good fit for? What industries? What experience, knowledge, and expertise do you have that is particularly valuable to them – and why is it so valuable?

**Actively conduct due diligence on the company you want to join**

After knowing your own strong points, do the reverse by conducting due diligence on the company. Below is a list of basic items to research:

Check all the signed reports that are prepared generally for the governing body or the team of board members of the company.

Read all the signed resolutions of the committee, including the written copies of the notices and all the paperwork details of the shareholders, partners, and the members of the company.

Review all the press releases and news that are issued by the organization or are relevant to the organization.

Inspect a complete summary of the personal relationships, business relationships, and affiliation details of the company's customers, shareholders, members, etc.

Know more about the business structure and strategies of the company, including areas where the business needs to expand or where you can use your knowledge skills.

Research skills and capabilities of the current officers and board members.

# What is a startup advisory board and what factors should I consider before joining a startup advisory board?

Many startups also consider creating an advisory board. An advisory board offers advice to the CEO or to another executive that runs the company. An advisory board offers business insights, expertise, industry knowledge, or experience. An advisory board also assists with other important business transaction decisions. Consider factors below in assessing startup advisory board opportunities.

**Familiarize yourself with board members**

What people are already included in the board of directors and advisory board? Do you know them? If not, you need to learn more about them and their roles. Eventually you may have to create a rapport with them. Make sure you know the people you will be working with and what they do. This will help you work more effectively and efficiently.

**Identify with the company's values**

You should have an idea of what the company is all about. What are its goals, mission, and plan? Does its niche interest you? What value will it add to your personal or professional life? This will be a key determinant in deciding whether to join a startup advisory board.

## Determine compensation

Advisory board members may be paid in one way or the other and it is important to understand what that means. For the first few years of the company's life, expect payment through equity of the company. If you were expecting cash, then your reasoning may be not be in line with the startup's objectives. If this is a problem for you, you should be prepared to have a conversation about it, likely with the CEO. Depending on your involvement with the startup and its industry, it is not unusual for a startup advisory board to award up to 1% in equity.

## Consider possible challenges

Every company has its challenges – including startups. But that does not mean you should not join a startup advisory board. It means that you should carefully educate yourself about the advisory board opportunity you are considering. When you have an advisory board offer on the table, it is a good idea to research and think it through to ensure your fit in light of your experience, expertise, availability, and relationship with other board members.

# How are startup board of directors members compensated?

If you are wondering how startup board members get paid, well, here is the *theory* behind it. Board members receive compensation for their roles in a startup business, but there are unique factors that influence compensation. These are normally related to time commitment, expertise, experience, knowledge, and other factors.

## Equity for compensation

It is not unusual for startup businesses to lack money to throw at the board members! So, after establishment, board members are more likely rewarded in the form of equity. At the early stage, board members should be looking at up to 1% equity, based on time commitment, expertise, experience, knowledge, and other factors. As the company grows and becomes financially stable, equity compensation rates drop and are replaced by cash. Even startups that have raised plenty of money often offer equity-based compensation of around 0.25% - 0.75%.

## Engagement level and compensation

Another major factor affecting the compensation of startup board members is how involved a member is with the company. There are three different levels which are high, medium and low engagement levels. Highly engaged members are more involved. They should expect the highest pay amongst the three categories. For medium engaged members, they lie somewhere between active and semi-active. Their compensation is also moderate. Finally, the lowest compensated are members who are less engaged. They are present and accountable for board meetings and often communicate through calls. They are not less important than the other board members, but their compensation is lower compared to the other two categories.

Although equity and engagement are the two main factors, a startup board member's compensation also depends on their experience, expertise, and knowledge. Popularity of the board member in the business world may also affect their compensation.

# What is a family business and what kind of board opportunities does a family business have?

A family business is owned by an individual or family, often consisting of two or more generations. The ownership lies in the family and the generations to come. Achieving success with a family business may become challenging as the family and its wealth increase.

There are several board opportunities that a family business can provide. Board opportunities at a family business are based on four different kinds of governance models. They include: compliance boards, insider boards, inner circle boards, and the non-influential board.

Compliance boards are meant to comply with laws and regulations set on business. The family can decide to appoint someone, either a family member or someone outside the family, to serve on the company's compliance board.

On insider boards, it is all about the family – no outsiders allowed. Each family member is given a position and they are responsible for ensuring they play their part for success of the family business. The leadership of an insider board will change with different family generations. The inner circle board is partly family and partly friends. It is often a one-person affair where the company's CEO selects people who are trustworthy within their individual inner circle. All three of these board structures are associated with and influence the company's chairman of the board in one way or another.

To get rid of that influence, a family business can choose to take a different direction. The non-influential board is made up of outside directors that have no association with the CEO. They are indifferent to personal matters and they work professionally. These directors bring their insights to the company's board and each one expects that their opinions will be regarded. As a result, transactions are more corporate and business deals are made solely to make the entity prosper. The non-influential board has immense benefits on a family business, precisely because the directors have no direct ties to the company.

# What can I bring to a family business board as an independent director?

Independent directors can do a lot to add value to the family business board. In fact, hiring directors that have no relationship to the business or the family has incredible advantages. Comparing the board of a family company to that of a public company, you will note that the former is more flexible. This is because they are free of U.S. Securities and Exchange Commission (SEC) regulations and stock exchange listings rules that must be adhered to by public companies. Once a family embraces an independent board of directors, they may include them in many, if not all, company matters. This may lead to a very hands-on board experience that some former or retired executives crave. As an independent director, there are many ways you can add value to a family business.

## Operations and risk management

Every business – including family businesses – needs a board of directors that has operations experience. Most family businesses do not understand how to understand operations in the simplest manner possible. As a director, you may provide necessary data and benefits to help the company's executives run a smoother operation.

This also related to risk management. All companies, public or a family business, are prone to risks. As an independent director you may be well positioned to flag, address, and mitigate various risks. The independent board of directors may offer solutions and techniques to control risks.

**Significant skills and assessment**

A board of directors may provide the missing skills to facilitate the company's success. Family businesses may not create a diversified board, especially because inner circle boards that are made up of family members and friends. This can be a problem because diverse boards are important for business success. However, by creating an independent board of directors, a family business can attract directors with diverse skills, knowledge, expertise, and experience to improve the performance of the company.

**CEO evaluation and succession debates**

CEOs are not always hands-on, or they may not have the right knowledge, experience, or expertise. Under such circumstances, independent directors may add value. As a director, you may have knowledge, expertise and experience on the different business aspects and you can advise the CEO.

Similarly, sometimes the next person in line for family business succession is not the best choice. They may have little knowledge in the nature of the business, not be interested, or need orientation prior to being affirmed the new company president. Independent directors can help the outgoing CEO choose the best successor for the business.

## Participating in corporate strategy approval

Developing the corporate strategy for a family business lies on the hands of the company's leadership and managers, most of whom may be family members and friends. However, before implementation, the board needs to discuss and approve strategies. This is where the independent board of directors may add a lot of value. For every goal a family business wants to achieve, members of the board of directors may know what is right for the company and strategies. Due to their diverse experiences, they may also know better ways to achieve different goals. Without an independent board, family businesses may face the issue of different agendas, which can result in a poor choice of strategies.

## Important investments and transformational transactions

As an independent director, you may be well-positioned to differentiate between valuable and bad transactions and investments. Based on your experience, expertise, knowledge, and connections you may help the CEO and family business leaders to enter better transactions and make more sound investments.

## Monitoring company performance

Once the corporate strategy applied to the company's performance, there needs to be a follow up and monitoring. That is also where an independent director may add value by inquiring about the progress.

## Influencing company behavior to the community

The success of a family business is also dependent on its behavior in the community. The services they offer may be part of the larger community where they live and hire their employees. Therefore, it is only right to give back and be involved in the community. As an independent director, you may be in a good position to build community relationships, serve as an ambassador, and generally help the company to grow a positive reputation in its immediate community and beyond.

## Managing external communications

Finally, you may be well-positioned to help with external communications. Shareholders, investors, family members, industry insiders, regulators, and authorities are all part of the bigger picture, and maintaining a great line of communications with them is paramount. This is where the guidance from an outside director maybe very valuable.

# What are advisory boards and why should I serve on them?

An advisory board is a group of people who give non-binding strategic advice to the boards of a company or organization. The nature of the advisory board is informal and flexible. Although an advisory board has no role to interfere in cooperative matters, they may serve as great recognition of one's skills and provide opportunities to network. Occasionally, serving on an advisory board can be a stepping stone toward larger roles including leadership roles and board service.

**The examples of advisory board:**

While there may be others, below is a list of example of advisory boards. Ultimately it is up to a company to decide what advisory board to form and how to run it. There is a lot of variation in how and why advisory boards are created and operated. Therefore, you need to do a lot of due diligence and understand all your potential commitments and obligations before you join.

**Risk advisory board**

The role of the risk advisory board may vary from company to company and depending on the scope of the business. The main role of the risk advisory board is to bring people together for risk management. The risk advisory board can also help the board, company leadership, and numerous other company stakeholders in making strategic decisions.

**Environmental advisory board (EAB)**

Environmental advisory boards tackle social and environmental responsibility. The EAB reviews the new strategies that other boards are planning to ensure that the company's actions don't harm the environment. In some companies, they also advise boards to come up with sustainable products and use products which are eco-friendly.

**Innovation advisory board**

This is a new way to address any product and innovation made by the company. The innovation advisory board helps the company create new innovations which are more beneficial to the company. This board also helps to improve the design of new innovations and gets them trending in the market. This particular advisory board help sustain the company's competition in the market.

**Technology advisory board**

The technology advisory board helps to upgrade the technology of the respective company. A technology advisory board often recruits young, talented members, who may not be hired as regular employees due to their very high salary expectations. This role involves an understanding of social media, data analytics, and mobility, which are the main topics of today's technology advisory boards.

Advisory boards may have a lot to offer you if you are able fit in. The advisory board team has a wealth of expertise that can help you to enhance your decision making skills and develop your network. Serving on an advisory board can also provide an opportunity to work on cutting edge problems. Below are examples of five ways an advisory board can create value for a company or organization.

**Walking the walk**

Advisory boards provide you with social, creative, and intellectual capital. The members focus on specific issues and may be valuable evangelists for a company or organization.

**Minimizing the risk**

Advisory boards play an important role in risk mitigation. Due to their knowledge, experience, expertise, and connections they may be a valuable risk mitigation and prevention resource.

**Staying ahead**

Advisory boards are usually composed of subject matter experts and industry leaders. Therefore, they may be helpful for a company or organization to stay timely and relevant.

**Anticipating the next big thing**

Similarly to staying ahead, the advisory board members may help to anticipate the next big thing, especially as part of the technology advisory board. After all, technology is transforming all industries around us.

**Opening doors to new networks**

Members of advisory boards can help secure opportunities in other industries and geographies. They may help consumer businesses to develop a business product and business facing businesses to develop a consumer product.

# What's the difference between a board of directors and an advisory board?

A board of directors, also known as the governing body of the institution, company or organization, is a group of individuals that are normally elected as, or elected to act as, representatives of the stockholders to establish corporate management related policies and to make decisions on major company issues. The board of directors' key purpose is to ensure the company's prosperity by collectively directing the company's affairs, whilst meeting the appropriate interests of its shareholders and stakeholders.

Normally, under the law, only governing board members and officers hold fiduciary responsibility to the institution, company or organization where they serve. Fiduciary responsibility entails three particular duties to the institution, company or organization where they serve. These are commonly known as the fiduciary duties of care, loyalty, and obedience. The corporate board of directors may be present in both for-profit and nonprofit organizations.

In contrast, an advisory board is comprised of a few individuals whose work is to provide advice to the CEO, other executives, or senior managers of the institution, company or organization in order to ensure the effective functioning of the company. Usually these are appointed, not elected roles. Most importantly, the members of the advisory boards do not owe a fiduciary duty to the institution, company or organization where they serve.

In addition to these key distinctions between a board of directors and an advisory board, the following may also apply:

**Terms, conditions, structure, and code of conduct**

A board of directors follows very strict terms, is elected at a certain regularity, has fiduciary obligations to shareholders, must abide by strict laws and regulations (e.g., SEC, NYSE, NASDAQ) and follows a prescribed strict code of conduct.

In contrast, advisory board opportunities tend to be more flexible, less regulated, require fewer terms, and almost never impose fiduciary obligations to shareholders.

**Responsibilities and working**

A board of directors generally advises across disciplines, subject matters, geographies, and problems. They tend to focus on all material issues that may affect the long term returns for company's shareholders.

In contrast, the advisory board tends to be much more specialized on a certain subject matter or problem. Therefore, its involvement tends to be much more limited in scope and duration.

## Influence, power, and voting rights

There is a major difference in the voting powers of a board of directors and an advisory board.

The members of a board of directors are the governing body in their institution, company or organization. They have a superior position in the company, with ample powers resting in them. A board of directors has the legal right to create or alter certain decisions and directions of the institution, company, or organization.

Advisory boards is less influential and powerful. They advise the CEOs, leaders, senior managers, and the board of directors in certain perspectives. However, the CEOs, leaders, and senior managers do not have to take this advice. It is completely voluntary for the management to follow an advisory board's advice. In other words, if the advisory board's advice is not followed, there is nothing an advisory board can do in terms of enforcement.

# 3. Why serve?

Board service may not be right for everyone. There's no shame in ultimately deciding to postpone or not pursue board service. This section focuses on reasons to serve on a board of directors. It also covers the risks of board service, as well as important questions to self-evaluate whether board service is right for you.

# Why should I serve on a corporate board of directors?

Board of directors opportunities may be powerful. They may add value to your resume, boost your experience level, provide opportunities to grow, allow you to work on challenging problems, let you set corporate strategy, help you raise a public profile, provide opportunities to influence, empower you to make important decisions, and much more.

There are several reasons why many professionals are increasingly considering board of director opportunities. The benefits of serving on a board of directors can hardly be ignored by anyone who is aspiring to take their career to the next level. Some of these benefits include:

## Intellectual challenge

Intellectual stimulation is the primary motivation for many professionals who choose to join a corporate board. Strategic planning, planning for CEO succession, navigating mergers and acquisitions, and many other milestone events are learning-rich opportunities, whether or not you have been involved with them before.

### Gain more expertise and experience

As a member of a board of directors, you may learn to handle complex issues from different angles and under different circumstances. You will also gain more industry experience.

### Grow your network

In addition to new knowledge, experience, and expertise, your network may grow substantially as a director. You will get a chance to build a network with fellow board members, investors, partners, industry thought leaders, CEOs, competitors, vendors, and many others.

### Develop your career

Serving on a board will also give you an opportunity to be in a strategy role without being consumed by daily execution realities and challenges. This provides you with more time to develop your career from a different, more strategic angle.

### Additional income stream

Serving as a board member, especially at a large public or private company, may offer substantial compensation. Although there is a lot of variance in compensation depending on experience, industry, company size, and many other factors, total compensation often has both cash and equity components and may be substantial.

## Be a leader

Serving on a board may increase your leadership abilities. In fact, you may find that other opportunities come to you as a result of serving on the board of directors of a company. For example, you may get other board opportunities, interesting job and consulting offers, and opportunities to speak. You can also be seen as an industry thought leader and enjoy an increased public profile.

## Understand board governance

Serving on a corporate board will most certainly increase your corporate governance knowledge and help you to become more fluent in navigating the boardroom, C Suite, and various important relationships. Just like most things in life, being comfortable navigating a boardroom comes with time and experience.

Ultimately, corporate board service is a gratifying experience that many professionals find rewarding and lucrative. It is absolutely worth considering, preparing, and obtaining!

# What makes board service a great leadership opportunity?

When filling a board of directors, most companies look for someone who has a lot to offer in terms of leadership qualities and experiences. Yet serving on a board of directors also provides an opportunity for professionals to further develop leadership skills and take them to the next level.

The board of directors needs performance, not just promises. Board members need an open mind, curiosity, and integrity. They need problem-solving and crisis management skills, as well as the ability to readily adjust with changing circumstances. They also need motivation, especially newer members, to bring out the best in others.

Therefore, it is very important for a board member to realize that leadership opportunities are not all about running the company. Leadership in the board context is also about setting a direction for executives and senior managers who in turn can guide employees.

In order to grow as a leader and be well positioned for board opportunities, it is helpful to develop these key skills as soon as possible:

## Get used to regular involvement

Boards are looking for someone who is regularly involved, has had hands-on experiences, and is committed to attending all meetings in person. In fact, regular meeting attendance is considered as a mark of excellence by most boards of directors.

## Build board of directors skills

Understand what a board of directors does, how their role differs from executives, and how to create efficient consensus among senior professionals from different backgrounds. These and many other skills should be developed throughout one's career.

## Build a wide and deep network

Many board members bring the value of their wide and deep network. Therefore, it is worth developing a deep and wide network throughout your career. Once you get on your first board, you should continue building your network even more to help bring you other board opportunities. In fact, one of the best rewards of joining a board is having better networking opportunities. These increased networking opportunities allow you to get connected with people who will contribute positively towards your development.

## Proactively build your reputation

Prospective board members who have spent a lifetime of building a positive and strong professional reputation in certain industries are an asset for any board of directors. Make sure that you proactively build your reputation and credibility over time. People will begin to see you as an expert and authority in your field of discipline, which will bring you opportunities over time.

## Strengthen your skills, experiences, and expertise

Of course, substantive skills, experiences, and expertise are valuable to companies looking for prospective board members. It is important to build your skills, experiences, and expertise throughout your career. This enables you to become an expert and provides you with opportunities for growth, including serving on corporate board of directors.

# Cultural awareness: what is it, why is it important, and how can I leverage it?

As globalization has become the new normal, the corporate world has also seen an increase in cross border recruitment, transactions, sales, exchanges, partnerships, and much more. Many companies are intentionally looking for board members who can represent global opinions and problem-solving in the increasingly competitive corporate world.

Many academics and business analysts have given their own definitions of "cultural awareness." Fundamentally, cultural awareness is the foundation of communication. It involves the ability to standing back from ourselves and become aware of our cultural values, beliefs and perceptions. It may include one's ability to recognize cultural, behavioral, historical, and philosophical differences.

Depending on the company you are considering, cultural awareness may be an important skill for serving on the board of directors. It is important to hone this skill throughout your professional life.

## What skills to develop

Have knowledge and self-awareness not only about your own cultural background, but also other cultures around the world.

Be open to the thoughts and beliefs of others and practice a non-biased approach when tackling various business issues.

Be open to communication where the flow of ideas is not restricted and barricaded by cultural differences. Communication is the key to cultural awareness.

Be adaptive to all kinds of situations, including those that are unfamiliar.

## How to leverage cultural awareness skills to get on a board of directors

### Be social

Socialize with the team. In some cultures, it is emphasized that everyone gets to know each other well before they start to work with each other. When a new member is introduced to the organization, there is often a welcome party, which is the best time socialize and get to know each other before beginning serious work.

### Know about local business practice

Every culture has its own set of values. It is important to know them and practice them. This shows that you are not only here to do business, but you are actually adapting to the work tradition. Examples can include practices related to business cards, greetings, and lunch.

### Settle on common grounds

It is not possible for everyone to have the same approach to all business strategies. No two countries have the same working conditions. At times, you will have to understand the economic background and tactics of other parties in order to effectively tackle the issues. It is important to emphasize common ground rather being rigid and firm on issues.

# What are the major questions to ask myself before joining a board of directors?

In order to assess your board readiness, it may be a good idea to ask yourself a series of questions before you begin your corporate board of directors journey. Below are some questions that will help you self-assess your board readiness.

**Why do I want to become a member of a corporate board?**

What actually compelled you to serve on boards generally and to this company or organization specifically? What is the reason that you are a good fit here? Try to narrow down why you want to serve this specific organization. Why do you want to associate your reputation with it? What value will you bring to the company or organization? In order for the relationship to be sustainable, the beliefs and the values of the company and organization must echo your own and the association must be mutually beneficial.

## How passionate am I about this organization or company?

A quality organization deserves and needs a passionate board of directors who genuinely contribute to the company's objectives and inner workings. A board of directors is not for those who simply take up space. Ask yourself how passionate you are about the organization's vision and objectives. Never take a director position just to look good or add some perceived value to your portfolio. If your heart and your mind are not in it, it will not be beneficial. Serving on a board is a big commitment and time investment that you should take seriously.

## Am I a complete match with the company's vision, mission statement, and core values?

On a board of directors, you may not be involved in daily execution and management. The privilege of sitting in the director's chair is to raise your voice to make a positive difference. Your role on a board of directors is to guide the organization and its leadership to stay on track and thrive. You can only do so when you are aligned with the company's mission statement, vision, and core values. Ensure that you have an in-depth understanding of the organization's vision, mission statement, and core values. Gather valuable input from all levels of the organization, including board members and leadership.

## Do I understand and embrace the organization's history?

Once you serve on a company's board, it is now your business. You need to understand what the organization has gone through the in the past as well as the current landscape and direction. Research recent staff changes and compare forecasts to reality. Audit statement history, projections, timelines, previous performances, public records, and word of mouth news. The organization's past may be the looking glass into its present and future, so take advantage of it.

## Are there any negative issues with the organization? If so, have I concluded that I can be effective? Are we really a good fit?

Insist on honesty and transparency from the start. You can never serve a company optimally if some points are left unchecked or in the shadows. Ask tough questions and make sure you get intelligent and timely responses. Create an expectation that you will ask and address the tough questions. This is the time and place to be transparent and act with integrity.

# What are the risks that come with serving on a corporate board of directors?

Before joining a board it may be a good idea to pause and consider how you can mitigate any potential risks. Below are some questions you should ask yourself in order to assess the risk profile of a board service opportunity and your risk tolerance. It is worth considering these questions both before you join a corporate board of directors, and periodically after you join.

## Does the company have comprehensive D&O insurance coverage?

Every company needs comprehensive directors and officers liability insurance (also known as D&O). As a first step, it is a good idea to know what the insurance policy covers and to what extent. It may also be a good idea to work with a professional to get you comfortable with the policy. Of course, a D&O policy doesn't cover all the risk factors. You need to do due diligence and weigh all factors in comparison to your own risk tolerance.

## Where are the risks of joining this company or organization?

If the stock price sinks, the directors can be sued – this is normal and completely expected. In fact, public company directors should be comfortable with this reality. It is the responsibility of the board to maintain financial strategies and manage sales and marketing plans. Directors can be questioned about the process of their decision-making at any time. Therefore, a board member should understand corporate governance, perform their duties diligently, engage in a good decision making process, continually educate themselves about the risks of their business, and work closely with legal and other professionals.

## Will joining this company or organization increase my reputational risk? If so, to what extent? How will I mitigate these risks?

Bad board actions or decisions may affect the reputations of its members, even if you were not involved in the decision or it predates you. As long as you are part of the board, people may have reasons to question your credibility and judgment.

Your insurance won't cover reputational risk if you are serving on a board as a director. And the damage to your reputation can be very costly and often irreversible. Only your due diligence may reduce the chances of your reputational risk.

Reputational risk is not at all new for corporate organizations. However, in today's digital age, news of the risks spreads faster than ever, reaches everywhere, and can be impossible to delete or contain. The reputational damage a director suffers may be severe and long lasting.

Therefore, it is important to understand and learn as much as you can about the company – where it has been, where it is, and where it is going – before you join as a director. It is also important to learn as much as you can about the company's current board, its executives, its founders, its investors, and its numerous other stakeholders.

**Is there a criminal risk associated with joining this organization or company?**

The chances of criminal risks are very rare for the board of directors, especially in the United States. You will find these kind of incidents only in the most egregious fraud cases. Of course, your due diligence about the company and its stakeholders should help you identify the main criminal risk red flags. You should also be alert and keep your eyes open once you join the board

## Is there a financial risk associated with joining this organization or company?

Generally speaking, the financial risk of serving on a board in the United States is low, provided that you follow established corporate governance rules along with any company-specific rules. To this end, understanding the company's charter, bylaws, other corporate documents, and corporate governance is important.

It is also important to understand how you are compensated. For example, what percentage of your compensation may be in equity that you are expected to not sell while still serving as a member of the board?

## Is there a cross border risk associated with joining this organization or company?

In the United States, the risk is generally low. Moreover, D&O should cover cross border risks. Of course, you may want to look more closely at the enforceability and the language of the policy.

# 4. How to get on a corporate board

A large part of your board journey requires getting board-ready. You will likely spend just as much time strategizing and improving yourself as a candidate as you spend actually pursuing and interviewing for specific positions. This section outlines the process of getting board-ready, from developing key skills to identifying board positions.

# What should I consider before deciding to serve on a corporate board as a director?

Board service was historically a part-time commitment for retired executives. However, this is changing. Corporate boards are increasingly open-minded about who they consider. Some of them are also rethinking their expectations from their board of director members.

Before joining a board, you need to make sure that you fully understand the organization's expectations and what it is actually looking for. To join a corporate board of directors you need to be sure that your skills, experiences, knowledge, and expectations are aligned with the company's expectations and requirements. Moreover, before finalizing your corporate board position you must know the correct corporate board position for you where you will be a successful director. The questions below are useful to consider.

**What and how valuable are your knowledge, expertise, experience, and time?**

How valuable is your time and expertise for various corporate boards of directors? Where do you add the most value? How valuable is your knowledge, expertise, experiences, network, and dedication? Use these factors to crystalize the value you bring. Why it is valuable? How valuable is it? Be very selective with how you use your time and expertise.

**What company can you benefit with your knowledge, expertise, experience, and time?**

Once you identify your unique value proposition, it is useful to zero in on who would most benefit from the value proposition you offer. Maybe you are well trained and knowledgeable about the fabric and the fashion industry, with a decade of operational experience in consumer athletic wear. If so, be prepared to research, identify, network, and approach companies and their stakeholders who may benefit from this value. If you are an experienced IT specialist in both the legal industry and business to business data companies, then you must figure out both narrowly and broadly speaking what businesses will find your insights valuable.

**Why do you want to serve on a board of directors?**

As with any undertaking, it is worth understanding your motivations and requirements. Below is a list of questions that you should consider asking yourself.

Why do I want to serve on a corporate board of directors?

What motivates and inspires me?

What industries am I passionate about?

Do I want to learn new skills?

Do I want the opportunity to hone my existing skills?

How will I make a difference?

How will this decision benefit my career or life goals?

What is my lifestyle and how does corporate board service fit into it?

In order to decide whether you should serve on a corporate board, you need to clearly understand and articulate the value you bring, who can benefit from it, and why you want to serve. That is, you need to define your goals, define your value, and identify the right organization for you.

# How can I choose the right board for me?

It is important to determine the right board for you and your experiences, expertise, and value before joining a corporate board. Otherwise, you may be wasting your talent and time. Below are some factors to consider.

**Inventory and understand your skill set**

To select the right board for you must first inventory and understand your skills. You need tp understand your knowledge, education, expertise, experience, and skills. Take time to reflect on your accomplishments, achievements, work history, education, businesses, and other milestones to make sure your list is complete. Then you can spend time identifying your most relevant board-related skills and matrix those that best communicate your value.

Spend time matching your skills, with both general industries and specific companies and individuals. Are your knowledge, education, expertise, experience, and skills a better match for private boards, advisory boards, nonprofits, or public company boards? Once you have an idea of where your skills match up, you can start considering the right board for you.

## Know and articulate the value you will bring

By joining a corporate board of directors, you must add some value to the company. The process of identifying and articulating the value you bring may take time. Here are some examples of what you may bring to the board:

Technology and risk mitigation for a consumer electronics companies

Nurturing new talent and managing talent across geographies

Finance and operation experience for food manufacturing companies

Sales or marketing experience and expertise for software as a service companies

Global commerce, export, and import experience for gas and petroleum companies

If you have transferable skills you can also consider serving on a board in a different industry to prove your skill across industries. Industries include:

Energy

Real estate

Technology

Financial service

Health care

Biotech

Software

Mining

Gas/oil

Entertainment

Gaming

Consumer goods

Retail

Consider what skills you have in your current industry that you can use to benefit others in similar, or related industries. It is important to consider all industries where your experience, expertise, and network may be relevant. Change your mindset and become versatile for corporate board positions.

**Diversify your interests**

Be more specific about what you are actually looking for in terms of company, responsibilities, compensation, and board experience. In the end, there is no objectively perfect corporate board position, just as there are no objectively perfect directors. Nonetheless, there are directors who are perfect for specific corporate board of directors opportunities. By being specific about what exactly you are looking for, you may realize that the best opportunity for you is one you haven't considered before.

**Enjoy the new challenges**

With a board of director position, you will have to face different challenges. It is a good idea to expect a learning curve. Be patient, both as you are trying to become a corporate director and after you join.

Appendix A provides an *Identify Your Target Board Opportunity* worksheet, which can be used to identify the right board service opportunity for you.

# How do I get a position on a corporate board of directors?

Getting a position on a corporate board is a matter of time, research, and skill matching. To land a board position, you must articulate your value proposition. To fulfill your goal you must follow these steps:

**Concentrate on your board resume and board biography**

Develop your board documents – your board resume and board biography – to jumpstart your corporate board of directors journey. A board resume and board bio are the most important documents of your corporate board of directors position search. These documents showcase your value by highlighting the skills, experiences, and knowledge that you will bring to the board.

**Define your elevator pitch**

In addition to your board documents, you need to be able to articulate your value in elevator pitch format. Because an elevator pitch is relatively short, you must be very selective in what you include and exclude. It may be a good idea to start with your board resume and board biography and reduce them to a few sentences that capture your value proposition. And of course, practice delivering your new elevator pitch! Delivering the pitch out loud can help you identify any changes you need to make.

**Network**

Many potential board opportunities come through word of mouth. Networking is acutely important to get a corporate board of directors seat. Start networking as soon as you identify your value and target companies/industries. Aim to meet board members, CEOs, chairpersons, and other professionals who are connected with a company's board such as attorneys, accountants, consultants, cybersecurity experts, and numerous others. Do not be afraid to be bold. Assure them about your value, skills, expertise, and experiences. Ask them what they can do to help you serve on a corporate board or if they can introduce you to those who already serve on or work with corporate boards. Be clear and specific – ask to be connected to with the companies that you think match perfectly with your value. Also ask them to introduce you to CEOs, chairpersons, and other relevant board-connected professionals at your target companies.

**Select a mentor and advocate**

Seek out a trusted person from your network, preferably one who serves on or is connected to a corporate board of directors. This person may share their ideas, advice, experiences, introductions, and knowledge. Sometimes this person may be at your current job, such as the CEO of your company. Others, however, may find it easier to have a mentor outside of their current organization.

**Consider joining a nonprofit board or advisory board**

Consider serving on nonprofit board or advisory board that you are passionate about before pursuing a corporate board position. This can help you to have some hands on experience, showcase your talents and expertise, and network. It can be a (relatively) low-commitment way to enter board service. Of course, make sure that you are truly passionate about the organization you are joining.

# What can I do now to become ready to serve on a corporate board?

Serving on a corporate board of directors is a challenging journey for everyone. You will need more patience and planning to start. Take the time to be strategic. Serving on a corporate board of directors is a huge challenge with great responsibilities. Even extremely talented, qualified, and experienced people often struggle to secure a corporate board of director seat.

**Here are some steps you can take now to reach your corporate board dream sooner:**

Give your 100% to your "day job" and always be at your best. In the end, you want to be the best business and P&L operator and have your skills and accomplishments recognized. To make yourself board ready, you need to achieve some success measures in your career. So, the very best way to have the position is to focus on accomplishing and succeeding in your own career.

Relevant operational experience is necessary to serve on a corporate board of directors. Seek out opportunities to gain this experience in your current position.

Being an expert in your industry may improve your visibility and reputation, which may be helpful in your corporate board of directors journey.

Start small to achieve something big: this is a secret of success in all undertakings. Consider starting with a nonprofit or advisory board to gain experience, expertise, exposure, and connections.

Be clear about your motivation, values, skills and reasons for serving on a corporate board of directors.

Keep in touch with professionals in your target industries, especially those who are considered experts, and those who serve on boards. Most corporate board positions are filled based on networking.

Do your research. A board member has considerable obligations and responsibilities. Make sure you understand how the boardroom works, what the law requires of board members, and where board members can get timely advice.

**Here are questions you should be able to answer if you are ready to serve on a corporate board:**

How much experience do you have as a senior executive leader in any private, public, or non-profit sector? A minimum of 10 to 15 years is a place to start.

Are you ready to work a minimum of 200 to 300 hours every year as a corporate board member in addition to your existing obligations?

Will you get the support of your current company's senior executives or other directors of the board for your new role? Are there company policies that will prohibit you from serving on a corporate board of directors?

At a minimum, are you comfortable and experienced in understanding and navigating a boardroom? Do you have your professional governance designation or certification (C.Dir or ICD.D) from any corporate director institute or college?

Do you have any nonprofit or for-profit board service experience in either a board member, observer, or board assistant capacity?

Can you work as part of a team by understanding the board's dynamics and by creating and following good governance?

What do you know about the liability, responsibilities, and functions of a corporate board director? Do you understand the risks of serving on a corporate board of directors? Are you familiar with ways to mitigate these risks?

Do you have the capability to maintain separation between a management role and the role of a director of the board? Will you be comfortable with determining high level strategy and letting the executives and senior managers run company's daily business?

Do you have the skill to at least proficiently understand and read financial statements regularly?

Are you ready to take responsibility for the critical areas of a company? Can you solve these issues with your prior experience such as digital media, risk management, M&A, international markets, cyber security, long data etc.?

# What are the characteristics and attributes of an ideal board member?

An effective and compelling board of directors requires powerful, effective, and collaborative individuals. Here are some of the key attributes of ideal corporate board of directors members:

**Passion**

Board members should work for a cause or organization that they are passionate about. This way they will be truly connected with the general mission and enjoy their corporate board service more.

**Experience**

Having the specific knowledge, experience, expertise, and skills that are valued by your target companies is the best way to be considered for board positions and enjoy your board service.

**Time**

Many individuals will consent to fill in as a member of the board without acknowledging the time commitment it will require. Besides standard meetings, there may be additional requirements to assume the responsibility of other tasks. Therefore, it is important to be clear about expectations and time commitments.

## Attentiveness

Board members must be proactive and not wait for issues to come to them. Board service requires individuals who can remain in front of the industry, their field, and their company's problems rather than continually being in a responsive and passive state.

## Toughness and collegiality

Board members must be prepared to go up against difficult and complex issues and go the extra miles through clashes. At the same time, they should be conscious and inspire mutual cooperation. Being able to balance these skills and seemingly conflicting values is an art worth perfecting. Be someone who is open to healthy arguments with others, but who can also eventually accomplish resolutions and keep a working relationship and connection in place.

## Highest level integrity and good judgment

A high level of integrity and a track record of good judgment are paramount for a corporate board member. After all, the members of a corporate board must make very important decisions, lead high profile companies, instill investor confidence, and help companies through transitions and important milestone events.

## Strategic thinking

Members of a corporate board of directors lead the company's strategy, which gives quantifiable objectives and goals for the company. The board member role is very separated from the role of daily management. It is important that directors are comfortable and proficient with setting and keeping an eye on a strategy.

## Preparation

Effective board members get their work done. They go to meetings educated and prepared to examine concerns and issues. They take the time to review and understand all important documents to administer effective strategies and objectives.

## Enthusiasm for learning and service

The most effective corporate board members are always ready to learn, cooperate, ask tough questions, and ultimately lead. They are driven and enthusiastic about serving others.

## Knowledge

Members of the corporate board of directors must understand the goal and mission of the company. They are acutely aware of where the company has been, where it is going, and how it will get there.

### Eye for diversity

A viable board incorporates and includes individuals from different fields and backgrounds, with diverse experiences, expertise, and knowledge, to guarantee that the organization is well-rounded in its qualities and strengths.

# How can I develop key skills to serve as a corporate board member?

To join a corporate board of directors, you need to identify the value that you bring. You need to emphasize your unique skills, experiences, knowledge, and achievements. The goal is to become more adept at precisely defining your specific skills. Below are a few ways to get there.

**Passion for a company, its mission, product/service, industry, and stakeholders**

As a corporate board member, you must be passionate about your company and its mission, product/service, industry, and stakeholders. This is required for members on both large and small boards of directors. Passion creates a drive in the corporate board of directors to succeed and overcome all obstacles. Heavily research the company and get to know its key players and stakeholders. Aim to make deep connections so you can develop a true passion for all aspects of the company.

**Decision maker**

Decision making is paramount for board members. A board member must be comfortable educating herself about complex subject matters where she has little or no expertise, making decisions by consensus, and coming to quick and accurate decisions in a crisis. Fumbling or getting confused is not an option. Working in different situations and organizations will provide you with a strong foundation to make decisions by consensus, and stay cool-headed, even in a complex situation where you are not an expert.

## Innovative thought

Corporate boards of directors set long term strategy and are responsible for the long term success of an organization. To this end, it is important to adjust to changes in the economy, foresee technological shifts, spot trends in your customers' tastes and preferences, and engage in out-of-the-box thinking in a strategic, calculated, and intentional way. Being open-minded and enriching your corporate board of directors with your innovative ideas is essential for serving your company.

## Staying active in your field and industry

Action is part of your corporate board service. While corporate board of director positions tend to be part-time positions, it does not mean they are part-time commitments. In fact, joining a corporate board of directors is a commitment to full-time, life-time learning. Whatever the value you bring to the board you must commit to further developing, refining, and upgrading these skills. Moreover, to set a long term strategy for your company you will need to understand and be involved in your company's industry and know key industry stakeholders. In other words, joining a corporate board of directors involves a sizable commitment in and out of the boardroom.

## Create long term strategy

Board members provide the strategic long term vision and strategy for the company, normally to maximize the returns for their shareholders. To this end, you may be making decisions that affect financial strategy, management strategy, technology strategy, innovation strategy, expansion strategy, and many other key decisions. Practice thinking in the long-term and understanding how different areas of a company interact. This can involve research, networking, and expanding your current position's responsibilities.

## Impeccable judgment, wisdom, and integrity

Boards are generally looking for people who not only have enough experience, but are also known for their impeccable judgment, wisdom, and integrity. After all, the corporate board of directors sets long term strategy for the company, leads all stakeholders, and inspires confidence in investors, government officials, and many other important players. Therefore, impeccable judgment, wisdom, and integrity are paramount. Ensure that your reputation in this regard is impeccable. If you are still in the beginning of your career, this can be especially useful to keep in mind.

## Diverse and relevant skills and expertise

Most decisions to fill a corporate board seat are at least partially driven by skills that a corporate board of directors may need given where the company is and where it is going. Therefore, it is very important to understand and articulate what skills and expertise you may be bringing to a corporate board of directors. Make sure that you develop a diverse array of skills to increase the chances that you are the "missing piece" a board is looking for. Also practice articulating your skills in flexible ways that show your value to a board. There is a difference between saying "I have legal experience" and "I am skilled at constructive risk analysis."

## Interpersonal skills and collaborative personality

Communicating and establishing a relationship with the other members of the board is a vital skill for a corporate board of directors to be effective and efficient. This is especially important for relatively large corporate boards because the decision-making process may already be slow and frustrating. Therefore, the skills of building coalitions, active listening, and choosing your battles wisely are crucial skills for any corporate board of directors member.

# How can I identify and address the skills I am missing to serve on a corporate board of directors?

Relevant skills are crucial for you to get a seat at the corporate board of directors table. You need to be acutely aware of the skills and experiences that you bring, as well as the skills and experiences that you don't have or don't have fully developed. You also need to be aware of the skills and experiences that your target companies need.

**Tips to identify and fill in missing skills**

**Highlight your core skills, experiences, and knowledge**

It is important to design your corporate board biography and resume in a way that highlights your core experiences, expertise, and skills. The aim is that you join the board of directors based on your core competencies and that the bulk of the interview process is spent in those areas. Discuss your skills, experience, and knowledge in measurable and specific ways to make a compelling case for that you are the ideal board member for the company that you are targeting.

## Research and identify the skills, experiences, and knowledge of the current board of directors

Consider what skills, experiences, and knowledge the current board of directors brings to the company that you are targeting. Similarly, what skills, experiences, and knowledge are missing? Can you fill in the missing skills, experiences, and knowledge? If so, you must highlight the skills, experiences, and knowledge that are missing from the current board of directors. To answer all of these questions you will need to do extensive research. For example, besides researching your target company and its specific needs and stakeholders, consider also researching the skills that the corporate board looks for when appointing a new director.

## Fill your experience gap

You will have to be honest with yourself and identify the skills that you are missing. If you are still a few years away from applying for your first corporate board of director position, consider taking strategic assignments and job positions to develop these skills. If you are already pursuing corporate board of director positions, consider highlighting the value and skills, experiences, and knowledge that you have, instead of what you are missing.

**Highlight your unique skills, experiences, and knowledge that are valued across industries, geographies, and companies**

Certain skills, experiences, and knowledge are universally sought after across industries, geographies, and companies. Some examples are foreign language skills, experience entering new markets, experience targeting new demographics, leading through difficulties and transitions, expertise in understanding and dealing with regulators, taking a company public, structuring mergers and acquisitions, facilitating post-M&A integrations, and changing company culture. Consider emphasizing these skills and experiences on your board resume and board biography.

# Generally, what factors are considered in corporate board of directors selection?

Generally speaking, the following categories of factors are considered when corporate boards of directors evaluate candidates:

Experiential attributes, such as education qualifications, accomplishments, industry experience, expertise, and knowledge, as well as functional experience.

Demographic attributes, which include generation, gender, geography, ethnicity, and diversity of thought.

Personal attributes, which include personality, interests, values, propensity to collaborate, judgment, integrity and cultural adaptability.

These categories of factors create a baseline that permits nominating board panels to more deliberately shape and improve the aggregate attitudes of the corporate board of directors. These factors are often addressed during the candidate appraisal process, either implicitly or explicitly, through interviews, meetings, references, psychometric examinations, and other evaluation techniques.

# How can I build great relationships that can lead to a corporate board of directors seat?

Finding the right board position for you is like gardening. You need to plant the seeds, cultivate them with care, and then harvest the fruits of your labor. Strategy, flawless execution, and timing are important. It is important to cultivate relationships that can help you identify or even connect you to board opportunities.

**Strategically expand your network**

Board service is all about relationships and networking. You must build your network to achieve success as a board member. And your network must be both deep and wide. Aim to regularly meet several people from the industry you are targeting. You should network with professionals who are respected in the industry or have connections to corporate boards of directors. You will need to go to relevant social gatherings, conferences, meetings, and other networking events. At these events be sure to ask for introductions. To get an introduction, contact people in your network or even those who are a few degrees removed.

You may have to contact some professionals whom you have never met before, have only met briefly, or haven't spoken to in a while. Although this may be uncomfortable, you need to persist and connect with them on regular basis. Show genuine interest in the person and what they do. Although not every new contact will lead to a board opportunity, the connections you make now will certainly serve you well when you are a board member.

Relationship building doesn't mean that you should only meet with directors, chairmen, and CEOs. It may be a good idea to build relationships with various other professionals who advise corporate boards, such as lawyers, consultants, and accountants. You may also seek out recruiters who work with corporate boards or help boards find new candidates, industry influencers, and numerous others.

**Intentionally participate in social media to showcase your skills, expertise, and knowledge**

Social media is an extension of your board biography and resume. LinkedIn is definitely a great place to start. Be sure to create a comprehensive profile on LinkedIn with your professional level details, skills, expertise, achievements, knowledge, and professional pictures. It is not unusual for companies to check out your LinkedIn profile well before they initially contact you about a corporate board of directors opening.

LinkedIn is also a great place to meet new professionals, including directors, chairmen, CEOs founders, service providers, and numerous others.

## Maintain quality relationships with other professionals

A professional relationship is different from a personal relationship. To build up a professional relationship consider following the steps below:

Be a good listeners. Nobody wants to feel patronized or used. Listen to what they are saying and ask questions to show interest. This is a valuable way to learn information about your target industry, company, corporate board of directors, and executives.

In preparation, research the person you are about to meet and her company. You can make a deeper connection if you can identify some common interest or background to discuss.

Consistently be helpful, generous, relevant, and timely in your offers, comments, and interactions. You can be persistent without being annoying. Make sure you offer to assist with the other person's goals as well – you may find that you can both help each other.

Share your specific goals and aspirations and ask for specific ways they can be helpful to you. Many people are happy to help others, but aren't sure how. If you can identify specific ways they can help, you can take the pressure off.

# 5. Practical steps to get on a corporate board

The board journey is an intentional process. You must be prepared with essential board documents and a high-profile professional reputation. This section will guide you through elevating your profile, using LinkedIn, crafting your board documents, and networking.

# How can I elevate my profile to get a board seat?

You must raise your profile to get your board seat. If you really want to become a board member, you have to work hard to become more visible. This can be a bit difficult but is definitely not impossible.

A good profile begins with a thorough self-assessment. Then you must determine your ideal destination and strategize a way to get there efficiently and effectively.

**Understand yourself and your motivation**

Clearly identify your purpose: getting a seat on a corporate board of directors. You also want to understand your interest. What drives you to serve as a corporate board member? How do you envision fitting this role into your life?

Also identify what industry you best fit into. You will need to have the necessary expertise in the industry you are targeting. If you are an expert in information technology or security, you can join an IT company or a company that will value this experience and expertise. An affiliation in your relevant industry is usually very helpful. Although you can pursue a board position across industries, it is very helpful to identify a baseline of where your "home" industry is.

Understand your target companies, their key stakeholders and decision makers. It is also useful to know their board hiring process and timing. Again, take time to examine your motivation and purpose. Why you are interested in these companies? How do you think you can add value to them in light of your skills, experiences, expertise, and knowledge?

**Consider your skills, expertise, experiences, knowledge, and education**

What unique value – skills, expertise, experiences, knowledge, and education – do you bring to the table? What are your superpowers? Which companies will appreciate your value proposition the most and why? What industries, stages, and geographic locations are these companies in?

In other words, know the value you can add to a corporate board of directors. Check that is the right time in your career to join a board. Ensure that you are a qualified fit for your target companies. Throughout all your outward interactions and communications, consistently prove that you can add unique value to the corporate board of directors of your target company.

**Prepare your corporate board of directors documents**

Your corporate board of directors documents should be polished and ready. It is important to spend considerable time developing and polishing them. And for many prospective candidates, working with another professional – whether paid or peer – can be helpful during this process. Another set of eyes can help you to articulate and refine you value, reach clarity, and improve your delivery.

For example, it is very important that a board biography helps evaluators quickly focus on the unique value that you bring to the table. Similarly, a board resume is different from other professional CVs and resumes. It must focus on the unique values, skills, expertise, experiences, and knowledge that you would bring to a corporate board of directors once you join. It must be polished, direct, and concise.

## Be social and use the most visible social media platforms

To raise your profile for a corporate board of directors position, make sure that your LinkedIn profile is a consistent extension of your corporate board biography and resume. If you don't have a LinkedIn profile, now is the time to create one – and fill it out as completely as possible. LinkedIn is an effective tool to gain visibility with your target company and its board of directors, chairman, CEO, and other executives and stakeholders. Depending on your industry and how social you would like to be, consider joining other social media platforms such as Twitter. The goal is to amplify your unique value consistently with your corporate board resume and biography.

Don't be shy! Self-promotion may seem unnatural, but it is important to embrace social media. Generally, corporate boards of directors are looking for a confident, respected and presentable professional. They are looking for leaders with good judgment and high integrity. If you want to join a corporate board of directors, you need a distinct, positive, visible, and memorable public profile.

There are many ways in which you can introduce yourself to the public. In fact, you should be very socially active in order to gain and maintain visibility. Here are some examples of how you can become active:

Publishing articles, blogs, papers, and books can help you to get noticed and cement your position as an influencer and leader in your industry.

Attending conferences, seminars, and meetups is a great way to network and stay on top of your industry.

You can also join NGOs, which are very popular in the business world, and volunteer for important assignments or events.

## Work strategically and intentionally

There are many professionals who work hard and hope to get noticed. But it's about working smarter, not harder. Getting credit for your hard work, both internally and externally, is as important as working hard. Choose assignments and jobs that fill gaps in your experience or increase your marketability. Make sure that your hard work is recognized, both internally and externally, so that your profile and reputation reflects your efforts.

# How can I effectively use LinkedIn?

LinkedIn is the most established way to raise your board-ready profile. Having the right LinkedIn profile – one that is an extension of your corporate board of directors biography and resume – reinforces your professional brand and boosts your opportunities, visibility, and overall presence.

Building up your network on LinkedIn is important because many corporate board of directors searches either start on LinkedIn or progress to LinkedIn profiles after the initial interest stage. Here are ways to optimize your LinkedIn profile:

**Activity and intentionally broadcast on LinkedIn**

LinkedIn allows you to change and modify your profile as much as you want. For example, you can add work experience or certifications and then broadcast these additions to your LinkedIn connections. If you take on an exciting speaking opportunity or start working with a nonprofit, make sure to update your LinkedIn profile and share the change with your network. This will give you an opportunity to shape your professional reputation and develop audiences around certain subject matters.

### Add relevant keywords to your profile

Add relevant keywords to your LinkedIn profile so that corporate board recruiters and others can easily find you in a sea of candidates. Give yourself some time to choose the right keywords first and then build your profile around them. This way you will stand out because you will more consistently show up in relevant searches.

### Update your profile photo

Set a professional profile photo on LinkedIn. It is the first thing that people see in your profile and you want to make a good first impression. Make sure that your picture is polished and projects the presence of a dignified corporate board member. It should not be a casual or low quality picture. Also consider adding other media – pictures, videos, press releases, and other links -- throughout your profile to add interest to your LinkedIn profile.

### Improve your headline

Update your "introduction" and headline to get more attention from recruiters and others involved in finding and evaluating board candidates. Your headline is located right beneath your profile name.

Use important keywords in the headline. Be sure to use the word "director" to signal your interest to serve on a corporate board of directors. Think of it as a very distilled elevator pitch!

# How can I position my skills, expertise, experience, and knowledge?

Creating your corporate director brand the best way to start your corporate board of directors journey. To create your corporate director brand you need your corporate board profile, biography, and resume. You must also engage in intentional due diligence.

**Board profile**

Your corporate board profile is a concise statement that clearly articulates your unique value proposition. A profile should be a summary of your overall achievements till date. It is a document that summarizes both your operational and personality details. Be sure to make it direct and written with complete sentences. Emphasize your skills, expertise, experience, qualification, knowledge, and achievements. Also emphasize important roles that you have filled, such as leadership roles or any role where you have made an impact. Highlight your collaboration and consensus skills. Avoid being too factual or using jargon. Write short, carefully crafted paragraphs so the reader will be inspired to ask for your corporate board biography and resume. The reader should be inspired to learn more about you.

## Board biography

A corporate board biography details your professional and board of directors experiences and accomplishments. Its goal is to provide a few more details in articulating the unique value you bring to the corporate board of directors. Use your profile as the framework ground when you create a corporate board of directors biography. The details in the corporate board biography must complement your professional profile. Include your work experiences, especially any board experiences (e.g. nonprofit or advisory board service). Also include relevant achievements and accomplishments. Normally the corporate board biography is one page. It has a brief introduction and then it highlights skills, major deals, experiences as a board member, skills, and your unique value. The goal of the corporate board biography is to keep the reader interested so that she asks for your corporate board resume.

## Board resume

Your corporate board resume is your corporate director portfolio that includes all relevant value, achievements, skills, expertise, experience, and knowledge. Use your traditional resume, but tailor it with board service in mind. A perfect corporate board resume should be based on facts about the achievements of your career. The goal is not to tell a story of your life but to strategically highlight qualifications, skills, experience, expertise, and your achievements. It should be a compelling story about the unique value you bring to the corporate board of directors table. Avoid overt self-promotion. Add your previous experience, the details of the companies where you have worked, and your specific and measurable accomplishments. Also add details about your academic history and other professionally relevant value. This includes achievements, skills, expertise, experience, and knowledge. Be sure to include your contact information so that others can get in touch with you.

**Perform due diligence and craft your strategy**

The corporate board of directors profile, biography, and resume are related documents and should be created together. They must hone on your unique value as a board member with increasing detail. Therefore, self-reflection and due diligence are an important part of creating these documents. Below are some steps you should consider in order to paint a more compelling story about your unique value proposition as a corporate director.

Do some due diligence to create your portfolio and cultivate your corporate director brand. You must present yourself as a valuable acquisition for the board by bringing value. Objectively examine your history, even aspects that you normally gloss over.

Have a targeted and fresh perspective. Gaining recognition is not easy. Your corporate director brand and value will be based on your current profile. You may feel that you are starting "from scratch."

Understand your strong points and the audience you are targeting.

Know your skills, expertise, experience, and knowledge and how to portray them as excellence. Focus your descriptions so they are targeted toward board service. Be very detailed and specific about your experience.

Identify and focus on your leadership qualities and progression but avoid overt self-promotion.

Look only for board opportunities where you will have the scope to prove your value. Aim for a position where your skills and personality are a match for the company and board. Sometimes the most "prestigious" seeming position may simply not be the right fit.

Your network is the easiest way to rebrand your career for board service. Meet more people personally and intentionally, both online and in person. Consider giving a speech at corporate gatherings or writing article in industry publications. This is an excellent way to create your brand through your valuable presence and skills.

# Why is a corporate board biography important, and how can I write one effectively?

## What is a board biography?

In general, a corporate board biography is a reflection on the leadership roles a professional has held throughout her career. It should not be confused with a CV or resume. A corporate board biography aims to express the professional's unique value, skills, expertise, experience, and knowledge. The format is more narrative than rigidly formatted.

## What to include in your board biography

### Work experience

Add your work experiences. Instead of simply listing company names and dates, describe major projects that you have taken up in your career. Detail your role in these projects and how you helped them succeed. It is a good idea to emphasize your leadership roles and strategic contributions.

### Business opportunities

Discuss the business opportunities that you have taken and how you followed through to success. Reading about your business opportunities helps others to better understand your potential and risk taking factor.

## Roles on technical teams

A technical person is recommended for hire more often than any other person in the professional world. Depending on the industry, it may be worth approaching your board biography from a technical point of view. Explain any roles you have held on technical teams for previous projects.

## Educational qualifications

It is essential to mention your educational qualifications in your corporate board biography. Educational qualification is the cornerstone of your career and often an important factor considered by board candidate evaluators.

## Useful tips to frame your board biography

## The heading should be "Biography for (Name)"

Underneath this title, briefly list your experience, leadership qualities, and interests.

## Mention your current corporate boards and advisory boards

Here, you should consider mentioning the companies or organizations of which you are currently a member.

After providing information about each organization, detail the roles you have held.

## List current board service

List any nonprofit boards or advisory boards you serve on. Highlight your responsibilities and accomplishments on these boards and any developments where you play a major role.

## Include major operating experience

Elaborate on the operating experience that you have gained throughout your career. Summarize your career from the beginning to its current point, with an eye for operational experiences. Emphasize your key skills, expertise, experiences, and knowledge.

## Detail educational qualifications

It is very important to mention your educational qualifications in your corporate board biography. Include any certificates or qualifications you have earned, not just standard degrees.

Appendix D features many sample board biographies and resumes. Feel free to use these as inspiration. Appendix E features a template that you can use to draft your own board biography.

# How can I choose a board opportunity that will boost my career?

Starting a career as a corporate board member can fuel your future by giving you more interesting opportunities. However, not every open board seat will be right for you. You must join a company that will complement your specific skills and management power.

**Search broadly**

It is intuitive to look for a corporate board position in an industry where you have at least some experience. Consider searching for opportunities in adjacent industries as well. For example, the industries of your vendors or suppliers may be offer a perfect place for your board service.

**Articulate your value fit**

Articulate what unique value you will bring to a corporate board. This can help you identify a board where you will be the best fit. You will often thrive on a board where your value fills a gap or provides a new perspective.

**Research and evaluate potential target companies**

Where is the company in its development? What challenges does the company face? Is the company expanding internationally? Is it involved in mergers or acquisitions? Where is it financially – does it need financing, is it winding down, or is it considering filing for bankruptcy? Is your target company small or large? Is it private or public? Is it a startup? Is your target company under close government investigation? Does it deal with regulators often? After researching the company, evaluate how this information fits into your specific corporate board brand. Do your skills, experiences, expertise, and knowledge position you to be helpful to your target companies? If so, how? You can add more value if you have had experiences with the challenges and opportunities the company currently faces.

### Consider serving on a nonprofit board of directors or advisory board

You can also start with a nonprofit board of directors or an advisory board. Although these opportunities may be very different from corporate board of director roles, they can present great opportunities to learn, network, and get started with board service – a all while you help a cause you care about or assist an exciting startup.

### Get to know activist investors

Get to know activist investors. An activist investor is an individual or group that purchases large numbers of a public company's shares and/or tries to obtain seats on the company's board with the goal of effecting a major change in the company. Activist investors may be looking for qualified director candidates that can be placed on a public board of directors. Before accepting a position from an activist investor, make sure you understand the specific activist investor, what motivates them, what outcome they want, and why they are interested in you for their target company's board.

**Start with small or private companies**

Don't go for the big, public companies at the initial stage of your board service career. Consider intentionally growing your board career over time. When you start out it may be a good idea to start your board service with a private company or a small public company. Then, as you gain skills, confidence, expertise, experience, and knowledge, you can consider whether you have the time, energy, and interest to pursue larger, more high profile public corporate boards.

# How can I network to get on a corporate board of directors?

You must actively network to get a position as a corporate director. Here is the general process of networking for a corporate board of directors:

You must first identify your target audience to set your plan and policies for networking.

Then identify individuals who you want to work with and build positive professional relationships with them.

Craft your unique strategy to get a board position. This is the most important step.

**Building a director-ready network is a process**

Meet professionals in-person at corporate gatherings, meetings, and conferences. Don't forget to also "meet" individuals through social media platforms such as LinkedIn. Don't be afraid to ask for help creating a strong, director-ready network. Try to meet professionals who have been in business for a long time and have achieved a lot of experience, skills, networking, expertise, and knowledge.

Landing a corporate board seat is actually both a contacts game and a numbers game. Be sure that your professional network includes all kind of professionals, including lawyers, bankers, consultants, and numerous others who serve a corporate board in any respect. Keep in mind that building a network takes time and that director-ready networks are both deep and wide.

## Create a process to network systematically and intentionally

To achieve a board position, you must network systematically and intentionally. You must understand the value of your network. Create a system to strategically and periodically meet, contact, and keep in touch with people who can bring you closer to your goal. For example, you can make it a goal to reach out to a specific number of contacts on LinkedIn per week, or attend at least three networking events per month. Make sure you also have a way to keep track of all your new contacts. Don't lose opportunities by simply forgetting to follow up or keep in touch with a valuable contact!

Appendix A provides a *Networking Plan* worksheet that you can use to visualize and strategize as you build a director-ready network.

# What is P&L and why should a corporate board member master it? How can I leverage my P&L experience?

## Meaning of P&L

P&L stands for "Profit & Loss" and refers to a comprehensive financial statement that is prepared at the end of a trading period to display the costs, revenue and expenses of a company over that period of time. It is more like a financial summary which shows whether a company has been able to make profit or loss over a given period of time. When the income is more than the expenses, profit has been made during that period, and vice versa.

## Why a board member should master P&L

### Better decision making

As a corporate director, you are involved in setting the strategy of the company, which means that your decisions are very important. Knowledge of P&L financial statements will help you to make more well-informed decisions.

### Analysis of revenue earning departments

Mastering the figures usually presented in a P&L statement enables a director to properly analyze the company's performance on a department-by-department basis. This allows you to identify departments which are underperforming and those that are living up to expectations.

## Projection of revenue

As a director, you must be able to know what to expect and how to set targets. The P&L figures are vital when projecting revenue.

## How you can leverage P&L experience

Understanding and being proficient in your company's P&L statement is crucial in your success as a director. Therefore, financial literacy is a plus for any corporate director candidate, even those that bring different talents to the company. Consider educating yourself about P&L and other financial statements in your current role. Take assignments where you are responsible for a large budget and have to make projections. Also consider volunteering for other opportunities that will increase your financial literacy. This can make you a more attractive candidate for board service.

# 6. Who can join a corporate board?

Board service is becoming an increasingly attractive career option. Although the traditional corporate board director is an ex-CEO or other high-level executive, professionals from all fields can leverage their skills to earn a board position. This section outlines how various professionals, from entrepreneurs to academics, can contribute to corporate boards of directors. This section also addresses younger professionals seeking board positions.

# What is angel investing? How can I leverage angel investing to join a corporate board of directors?

Angel investors (or "angels") provide a startup or early stage company with the required funds to start a business. Through the entire process, the role of an angel investor is vital. They offer the requisite capital with particular "terms and conditions" as the basis for their investment. As they are providing capital, they may also work as a mentor for a startup business.

**Role of the angel investor**

After diligence and investing, angels may informally or formally advise founders about numerous issues. Depending on their interest, expertise, skills, experiences, and knowledge, investors may play the role of a board observer. Although they may not have voting rights to make any major decision for the business, their opinion is highly valued. Occasionally, an angel investor may even join the startup's board of directors.

**Leveraging angel investing**

If you have experience as an angel investor, you can translate your skills to corporate board service. When discussing your angel investing experiences, highlight any impact you have made on a startup's long-term strategy. Also emphasize any operational experience you may have gained. Of course, if you held a role on the startup's board of directors or advisory board, this experience can also be leveraged to gain a position on a public company's board of directors.

# What experiences can lawyers bring to a corporate board of directors? What qualities should they emphasize?

There has been a continued argument about whether lawyers should be part of a board of directors or not. Lawyers can bring many experiences and skills to corporate boards of directors.

## Legal advice

Lawyers spend their careers advising and influencing specific issues and risks which may be affecting their companies. They give their independent advice on the options that a business may have. A lawyer can transfer these skills to board service to be a useful voice of reason for a corporate board of directors.

## Legal representation

Legal disputes arise for all companies. For some, they may even be routine. Lawyers are generally good at strategically managing and advising corporate boards of directors about navigating risks at various stages of legal conflict. Lawyers may add value to businesses that have a high conflict or litigation risk.

### Risk-management experiences

Lawyers also have experiences with managing risks related to procurement, contracts, patents, property, government regulations, international expansion, mergers and acquisitions, IPO, and numerous areas. Depending on their experiences, they may also have broad exposure to and management experience in legal and business issues. This can help lawyers provide a useful perspective to corporate boards of directors.

### Great communication skills

Lawyers spend a lifetime perfecting their communication skills in many settings and circumstances. They negotiate, mediate, argue, influence, educate, relate, advocate, and strategically communicate throughout their careers, all of which is an asset for corporate directors.

### Analytical skills

Corporate lawyers are skilled at deliberately learning, analyzing and interpreting various situations and risks. These are very helpful qualities for corporate directors. A lawyer on a board can help to structure a discussion in a more logical and systematic way.

### Researching skills

Proper research is a hallmark of legal education and practice. It is an essential foundation for managing risks and coping with uncertainty. Lawyers can help the corporate board of directors to research and educate themselves better. They can also be helpful in framing and re-framing questions for the corporate board of directors to focus on.

### Additional benefits of attorneys on corporate boards

Attorneys are experts at solving legal issues. They can decrease the chances of legal risks and enrich the team with their useful strategic tips. Other ways attorneys add value to corporate board of directors include:

Attorneys possess lots of intellectual qualities and skills to complement the other existing corporate directors.

They are comfortable handling the complexity of the corporate boardroom.

They can masterfully navigate major perspectives, legal issues, and ethical dilemmas.

Lawyers have the skills to analyze and address business challenges.

They can contribute useful insight and diversity to boardroom debates.

Lawyers can facilitate crucial decision-making in the boardroom.

Lawyers are trained and experienced in absorbing and analyzing large volumes of information and documents.

# Do academics qualify to serve on corporate boards of directors? What qualities should they emphasize?

Academics may play a role on a corporate board of directors. A reputable person serving on a corporate board of directors tells a lot about a company and its prestige and reputation. It is important for corporations to include directors who deeply understand the subject matter that is core to a business.

Academic leaders who have any cooperative or entrepreneurship experience, who understand real-world business outside the academic context, and who have important and relevant subject matter expertise may be very attractive to the board of directors.

**An academic may bring these qualities to a corporate board of directors:**

### Strategic skills
A board of directors is always in need of new strategies to take the business to a new level. Generally, most boards are looking for problem-solving skills, leadership qualities, strategic thinking skills, and an understanding individual. Depending on one's individual experiences and interests, an academic may already have these skills.

## Interpersonal skills

A corporate board of directors also wants a professional with good interpersonal and professional behavior. Academics may excel in discussing important and controversial topics and analyzing evidence to find the right answer. Academics may also excel at maintaining transparency in professional relationships and collective undertakings.

## Diversity

Diversity of thought is an asset for a corporate board of directors. Academics may bring much-needed diversity to a corporate board of directors. They can help the company evaluate different viewpoints toward relevant issues, strengthening its core operations.

## Experience

Usually companies look for experienced and mature directors, with an excellent amount of experience in the same industry. Academics can definitely can skills, experiences, expertise, and knowledge in areas where they have spent a lifetime researching, teaching, and publishing.

# Do entrepreneurs qualify to serve on a corporate board of directors? What qualities should they emphasize?

Entrepreneurs may be qualified to serve on a corporate board of directors. It is essential that an entrepreneur candidate has enough experience handling business opportunities.

**An entrepreneur may bring these qualities to a corporate board of directors:**

### Good business judgment

Good business judgment is the prime skill of every corporate board director. An entrepreneur's board profile, biography, and resume must demonstrate a track record of hiring good people, making sound business decisions, and overall good judgment.

### Knowledge and skills

Another essential point is that an entrepreneur should be knowledgeable about relevant knowledge, trends, practices, key stakeholders, and ethics. An entrepreneur's board profile, biography, and resume must demonstrate a strategic and technical point of view. They must display a track record of handling situations systematically. An experienced entrepreneur is most likely to have good judgment skills and great knowledge.

## Industry dedication

If the entrepreneur is highly attracted towards working in this company's field, chances are high that they can produce productive positive results. Being passionate about your work is the key to success. An entrepreneur's board profile, biography, and resume must demonstrate passion and long-term commitment to an industry.

## Unwavering focus

Entrepreneurs must be willing to devote time and effort to the organization. Many people are interested in getting on board but do not have sufficient time to be truly focused on a new organization. It is essential for every corporate board member to make a serious time commitment to their organization. An entrepreneur's board profile, biography, and resume must demonstrate unwavering focus and interest in their organizations' success.

# Do professionals with financial backgrounds qualify to serve on a corporate board of directors? What qualities should they emphasize?

Professionals with backgrounds in finance are definitely sought after for corporate board positions. Some companies even prefer candidates who are qualified by SEC standards as "finance-experts." The main role of any company's board of directors is to take care of the financial affairs of the company, which often means maximizing long term returns to shareholders. They need to keep track of the profits and costs and make sure that the company is growing and meeting its goals.

**Qualities that are emphasized**

Financial education and experience in the industry where the target company operates are very important. When choosing a board member with financial expertise, companies often emphasize:

**Work experience**

Excellent work experience is important, especially in the relevant industry, because companies prefer to hire board members with a deep understanding of specifically relevant financial issues. Companies, especially public companies, have historically preferred onboarding working CEOs or CFOs, especially those from Fortune 500 companies.

Have you held titles such as CFO, Treasurer, VP of Finance, Director of Finance, Director of Accounting, Director of Financial Reporting, Corporate Controller, Controller, Divisional Controller, or a similar title? Have you dealt with tax, compliance, GAAP, financials, modeling, budget, treasury, costs, SEC and other regulators, tariffs, audit, and similar issues? If so, make sure that your board profile, resume, and biography indicate the size of the budget you managed, transactions that you led, and milestones you achieved.

## Financial education

Relevant and current financial education, training, and credentials are important. Be sure to emphasize your finance- and accounting-related credentials and coursework. Also highlight any specific educational milestones. For example, if you are a certified public accountant (CPA) that is highly relevant information.

## Continue your education

Keep yourself updated about new financial requirements, especially those that affect your target industry or companies. Consider attending industry events that focus on finance and accounting impact. Network and keep in touch with CPAs and other finance and accounting professionals. Make sure you read financial literature, including books, newspapers, academic papers, industry white papers, and blogs. This way you can keep your hand on the pulse and stay conversant about important financial issues.

# Do private equity professionals qualify to serve on a corporate board of directors? What qualities should they emphasize?

Private equity professionals can be valuable corporate directors for many reasons:

## Understanding financials and operational mastery

Private equity professionals are sophisticated about finance and accounting and therefore would be valuable board members, especially if they have relevant industry experience. They may be very helpful in advising the board about the best ways to raise money and minimize related risk. They are also strategic in their thinking and execution. Their experiences are deeply rooted in the operational realities of a business.

## Mastery and management of investments

Private equity professionals may be well positioned to help companies that are involved in investments. For example, they may help manage expectations about expected returns or help structure investments to maximize returns. They may also help monitor company investments to ensure that their performances meet management's expectations. Finally, private equity professionals may be instrumental in helping the board to structure its strategy for acquiring or selling various assets.

## Superb experience, expertise, and training

Private equity professionals must go through a series of training and education. Therefore, many private equity professionals have consistently stellar education. Moreover, on-the-job training leads to superb experience and expertise and a high degree of financial literacy.

Do engineers and other technical professionals qualify to serve on a corporate board of directors? What qualities should they emphasize?

It is helpful for engineers and other technical professionals to be skilled in the arts and science that the target company practices to at least some extent. In addition to their substantive skills, engineers and other technical professionals may bring other value to the corporate board of directors.

A tech professional may bring these qualities to a corporate board of directors:

**Innovative ideas**

When engineers and other technical professionals are on the corporate board of directors, they may be instrumental in ensuring that the organization is moving with the times by bringing in new ideas to benefit both potential and existing customers. This helps a company stay innovative and competitive. It also helps companies recruit and retain technical and product talent.

## Quantitative skills

As expected, engineers and other technical professionals are often strong in math and science. This means that they also tend to be very good at understanding product-related or research-related quantitative information. They also tend to understand financial information and trends, comprehend large volume of quantitative data, and ask good questions.

## Practical reality of building a product experience

Engineers and other technical professionals often have education, training, skills, experience, knowledge, and expertise in building products and finding product-market fit. They may be useful to have on a corporate board of directors when a company considers launching a new product offering, changing an existing product offering, expanding its product offering to other geographies, acquiring other products to add to its portfolio, or dealing with technical regulators such as the U.S. Food and Drug Administration (FDA).

## Experience researching and building products

Professional engineers who have worked their way to a board position are often proactive in nature and have experience listening to customer feedback. This means that they have the knowledge and technical know-how to spot a problem and have it tackled in a professional way before it will even surface. They also can help the company listen and interpret customer feedback.

# When am I too old to serve on a corporate board?

Historically, the average age of a corporate director is a little over 60. To an extent this makes sense. Many companies want professionals with a successful career full of achievements, skills, experience, expertise, and knowledge to serve on their corporate boards. For the majority of directors, especially at public companies, board service is a career move after a successful and thriving career, often in the same industry as the company where they serve.

The age of directors (and their term limits) is a much-discussed topic in the corporate world. Ultimately, just like everyone else, seasoned professionals must articulate the answers to two fundamental questions: what unique value do they bring to a corporate board of directors, and what will they do to stay relevant?

## Wealth of experiences to articulate your value

Professionals with longer careers tend to have a larger wealth of education, training, experience, expertise, achievement, and knowledge that helps them to articulate their unique value proposition for corporate board of directors. They also tend to have a wider and deeper network of professional contacts and might have a historic perspective on a company or industry. They often command respect due to their achievements and age. Companies may consider age as an asset for corporate boards because age highly correlates with the attributes that many companies seek.

## Contrast with new thoughts

Yet every professional, of any age, who wants to serve on a corporate board of directors must articulate how they will stay relevant in an industry that may be changing quickly. How will you help promote new thoughts and understand new trends? How will you stay on top of your industry and profession? What classes or experiences will you seek? What books and periodicals will you read? What experts will you use to help you stay up to date? How will you educate yourself about the new technologies, developments, and trends? Regardless of age, it is important to understand your responsibility to stay relevant, active, and educated.

# Why should I start pursuing my corporate director career when I am young?

This is the era of new thoughts and ideas – and this has completely the business world. Young people are increasingly present on corporate boards because they bring fresh ideas, start new trends, and help overcome the boring persistence of old ideas. Young directors can enrich a board with their new thoughts and ideas and can fulfill the potential gaps of a growing business. As a young professional, your hunger, passion, and creativity will help you add fuel to you corporate board journey.

One of the secrets of a successful board is diversity of thought. A well-balanced board with different points of view, ages, experiences, strategies, opinions, and voices can better reach business goals.

Consider approaching corporate board service strategically and early. While it can be very daunting to start a career as a corporate director, especially at a young age, it may be a prudent approach.

Serving on a corporate board may be an amazing experience that goes along with (not after) your career. It may increase and enrich your opportunities, knowledge, skills, experience, visibility, and network. Consider these strategies to position yourself to serve on a corporate board relatively early in your career:

## Emphasize fresh ideas, new approaches, emerging industries, and cutting edge technology

In articulating your value to a corporate board of directors, consider emphasizing your fresh ideas, new approaches, experience in emerging industries, and knowledge of cutting edge technologies. Do you know the emerging market trends that many people miss? Do you understand how new technology will impact the industry, company, products, disciplines, consumer behavior, regulations, or supply chain? Make sure that you present these valuable qualities.

## Develop the broad thinking and leadership skills

Boards generally focus on planning and strategy, not minutiae or day-to-day operations. Seek experiences and assignments with broad roles, think strategically, and lead. Routinely ask yourself: Do my current opportunities give me the full picture? Am I progressing in developing my skills? Do I routinely participate in setting strategy? Am I part of the P&L discussion? Am I responsible for a sizable budget? If you sense that your current role is not preparing you for board service, seek out new projects that connect you with more strategic roles.

## Consider how board service may enhance your career today

Becoming a corporate director at young age will provide you with learning, growth, expertise, experience, and networking opportunities. Consider educating yourself about the richness of board opportunities – nonprofit, startup, family businesses, private companies, public companies, Fortune 500. Between nonprofit and Fortune 500 company boards there is a very rich middle ground of opportunities that most professionals don't know or appreciate. Understand how these opportunities are different, where you can provide value, and how they can go along with tour career. Board opportunities of all kinds may help you grow your career, boost your leadership skills, increase your expertise, provide new challenges, present opportunities to give back, and expand your network.

## Grow your network deep and wide

You are never too young to grow your network. You want to make sure that your network is deep and wide, composed of people from various disciplines, backgrounds, and perspectives. Consider including current board members, chairmen, CEOs, executives, founders, VCs, industry influencers, subject matter leaders, and numerous other professionals who work with boards of directors. This will give you a head start on your board journey.

## Embrace the digital age

The digital age is here. The Internet offers a wealth of opportunities to learn, acquire skills, and expand your network. Take advantage of numerous social platforms to start building your professional reputation early. What is your digital reputation? What are you known for? Do you regularly share content consistent with your reputation and values? Are you becoming an expert in a certain subject matter, industry, or geography?

## Develop an international perspective

In the increasingly global economy, a genuine understanding of international culture, market, environment, technology, entertainment, and trends is valuable. It also takes time to develop. You should start developing your world IQ and worldview early. Consider seeking out jobs and assignment with international responsibilities, networking with peers in your global company, traveling, learning about particular markets, and getting involved in international organizations and NGOs.

Appendix A features a *Board-Ready Thought Leader* worksheet that you can use to plan your board-readiness at any stage of your career.

# 7. Due diligence

Becoming a board member is a massive commitment. It is essential to make sure the specific board opportunity you are eyeing is right for you. Due diligence will help you identify the issues you may face as a director at a specific company. Ultimately, due diligence can help you decide whether a specific board position is right for you. This section explains how to conduct due diligence and how to evaluate the information you uncover.

# What are the right ways to research target companies for a corporate director position?

In order to get on a corporate board it is important to research your target companies. To do so effectively, you need to consider many sources of information.

**Inside sources of information**

Start with the information that companies generate themselves. Companies generate quantitative and qualitative information, both of which could be helpful in researching your target companies and preparing for interviews.

Quantitative inside information includes:

(1) financial statements, which are important to understand the current financial status of the company,

(2) financial statement footnotes, and

(3) stock valuation.

Qualitative inside information includes:

(1) reviewing the statements of financial prolixity, (2) attending or listening to conference calls, and (3)

reviewing material on the company website such as investor packets and presentations.

Furthermore, it is a good idea to review companies' SEC filings. Knowing their quantitative and qualitative information is necessary. Look mostly for the presentation consistency and work style of the company. Research on more basic inside information like how they face any question, how they answer a question in different ways over time, trustworthiness, and whether their performance proves their statements.

**Outside sources of information**

It is also important to review information that was not produced by the company. There are many outside information sources to consider.

Message boards like Yahoo can be a great resource. Message boards can help you understand trends. Customers, clients, and vendors also post complaints.

Consider asking people in your network, preferably in person, their opinion on the company. Generally, people don't like to put as much information in emails. People in your network will be more forthcoming on the phone or in person.

Another good option to get information is boards on Topix.com. This is an amazing option to get messages from average people and consumers. Although you may need to wade through the mass of content, browsing these boards can help you understand the trends and culture.

Another great way to get information about your target company is analyst reports. When you are interviewing with a company, ask for the analyst's reports. Look for the original reports. If they provide you with edited versions of the analyst report, that in itself is telling. Also, consider locating analyst reports on your own.

Another way to get information is Alpha and the Motley Fool reports.

Last but not least is Google. You never know what you will find!

# What should I look for during due diligence on a corporate board?

These factors can help you understand whether a specific board opportunity is right for you.

## Know everything about the company

You should research thoroughly about the company. Understand both the assets and belongings of the company, and the products and services that are provided by the company. For a proper subjective understanding, you should analyze the company's financial statements, stated objectives, and results.

## Values and perceptions

You should investigate what it is like to work at the company. Specifically analyze the values and perceptions the company follows and passes it to its employees.

Research professional ethical and legal principals at the company (or those that are missing from the company). Information from people with first-hand experiences is most valuable. Employees of the company can be asked for their reviews.

## Work environment

Investigate the company's work environment. What type of work environment does the organization offer? Is it good or bad? Research these questions. The work environment is a prime influencing character for recruitment and the company image.

## Goals and strategies

Companies frame goals every few years in association to fulfill their main objective. To analyze the performance and the success of an organization, you must understand the company's goals. Then you can identify specific projects that the company is working on and the strategies it is considering. Success or failure of the company in certain scenarios can also be noted.

## Analyze the potential of the board of directors and the CEO

Analyzing the potential of the board of directors and the CEO will help you evaluate the future success and scope of working of the organization.

The CEO and the board of directors are the core members of the organization. Decision-making and overall strategy are explicitly dependent on them. Assess the qualities of the CEO and board members and their skill at managing the organization.

# How can I conduct due diligence on a startup before joining its board?

Joining a startup's board of directors or advisory board may be very risky. Due diligence is an effective process to identify the major risks of being involved. If a prospective startup investor, board member, or advisory board member does not like everything they uncover in the due diligence process, they can take appropriate action. This can range from suggest a risk mitigation to the company, or backing out from the investment, or declining an offer to join.

Due diligence is a straight forward process that sounds overwhelming if you don't have an accounting or legal background. It is now more standardized. Below is a list of items to consider when you conduct a due diligence on a startup:

**Some due diligence documents are:**

**Overview on client acquisition channels**

It is helpful to request an overview of your potential customers and the lead funnel, along with information on the costs of customer acquisition. If you have access to a good report or case studies of potential customers, it may be a good idea to review these as well. Add a complete customer's list in the pipeline of the company's recent sales.

## Spreadsheet on key metrics

Consider reviewing key metrics, which your investors may ask for during the process of fundraising. For example, be sure to understand the company's users, revenue, cost of customer acquisition, rates of growth, lifetime value, runway, burn rate, and all the other core metrics of the company that you are tracking actively.

## Financial projections

It is a good idea to understand a company's financial plan for the next three years. What is a clear and expected financial scenario for the future of the company? Just like how investors carefully examine projections in due diligence, potential startup directors or advisory board members should engage in a similar exercise on a smaller scale.

## Financial and strategic reports

Before joining a startup board of directors or advisory board consider reviewing financial and strategic reports of the company with the details of every board member and other key people such as stockholders and vendors.

## Key legal papers

Consider reviewing key legal documents from foreign and domestic jurisdictions for the company such as incorporation, leases, assets, taxes, locations of employees, and others.

## Website and press releases

It is a good idea to review all the recent news, press releases, and website details.

# What are the red flags to look out for when searching for a corporate board of directors position?

You must go through intensive due diligence to join a board. Identifying red flags now will help you be successful in the future. Red flags are the places that the board of directors has marked to improve or change.

**Look for random and systematic risk**

Board members must identify the flaws and risks that can develop into hazardous issues for their companies. You can use your network to know the current incidents and status of the company.

**Watch out for auditor changes**

Another red flag is when a company changes its auditor. An auditor is responsible for making the annual data audit of a company.

**Pay attention to procedures and policies**

The board is responsible for making policies for its organization or company. Boards must have all the information about the policies and different procedures of the company. Each board member must read through them carefully and approve each policy before proceeding. There are various types of policies, such as policies for social media, emergency planning, and acceptance of gifts, Sarbanes-Oxley compliance, and more. Board members also need to identify the reason for missing policies – do the regulations not exist or are the policies still under cover? They should have all the info.

## Pay attention to board meetings

When do normal board of directors meetings for a company normally take place? Has the frequency of these meetings increased? If so, why? Were all board members and executive staff of the company present at the meeting? If not, what was the reason? What is the normal source of information for the board? Is the board depending on just one source to get the information, or is the board proactively educating its members using a variety of sources?

## Pay attention to financial information

Of course, it is critical to understand a company's past and current financials. Financial statements should be examined. Have the right financial reports been sent on time? Have they been viewed by all the board members? Each board member should be able to understand the statement in a board meeting. Is there any accounting method which can be only understood by the members of your finance department? Is there any responsible audit department for the company? Is there a departmental and organizational budget of the organization? Are the board members receiving timely reports on that budget?

## Miscellaneous red flags

Are the company's investment relations operated or communicated by a lawyer? Look for all the narratives and the profitability of the company. Are they consistent? Do they make sense over time and in retrospect?

# 8. Interviewing

As with any job, getting on a corporate board requires an interview. If you're pursuing board service, you have likely been through your fair share of interviews. But a corporate board of directors interview is entirely unique. This section covers what to expect at your board interview, what to do before, during, and after the interview, and what to look out for while interviewing.

# How can I leave a good first impression as a prospective board member?

Your first impression can either make you or break you completely. For a board of directors position, making a first good impression is not something that can be achieved in one day or within few hours. This is not something that can happen as a fluke! You need to prepare so that when the right time comes, you can make your move, shine, and ultimately get noticed.

## Experience

Companies are looking for people who have industry insights, experience, or expertise in fields where the company can benefit from making you a board member. You must know and articulate the value you bring to the table. What companies benefit from your background? What special experiences have you had? What doors can you open? What insights can you provide? Ultimately, what sets you apart and makes you a perfect fit for a specific board of directors opportunity?

## Staying current in your industry and field

Staying updated with the target company's affairs and industry is very important for the board of directors. This will not only make you aware of what is happening at the company but can also help you make a good first impression as a prospective board member.

## Continue learning

Be your own toughest critic and constantly evaluate where you are lacking in terms of skills, knowledge, and network. Join seminars, update your skills, and attend industry events and trade shows. Prioritize your learning and development and stay on top.

# What should I expect at a corporate board of directors interview?

## Interviews

At a minimum, the interviews of the board of directors are usually conducted by the chairperson of the board, the presiding or the lead director of the board, members of the nomination committee or the governance committee, and the CEO of the company. It is not unusual to also meet other board members and executives of the company.

The style, frequency, and length of the interview varies from company to company.

## Questions

Qualifications and you bring to the company should be consistently articulated during the interview. Your experience, achievements, knowledge, expertise, interests, and connections will ultimately set you apart.

Other types of questions will attempt to ascertain your ability to constructively collaborate and bond with other board members, executives, stakeholders, vendors, partners, suppliers, and their network.

## Questions to expect

What are your personal objectives and goals?

What value will you will bring to the company? How?

What strategies may you suggest for the company?

What do you know about the company and its unique history, position in the marketplace, and vision?

Why do you want to serve on this board?

How much experience do you have as a board of director?

What are you currently doing?

What skills do you have to serve the board?

What is a brief summary of your achievements and experiences?

What is your background?

How do you handle complex situations in your professional life?

How much time have you contributed to your current position? How much time can you can give to this organization?

How do you deal with conflict?

# What should I do before my corporate board of directors interview?

In order to make your board interview a huge success, make sure that you:

**Understand the company**

As simple as this may sound, many people fall short of this requirement. You must understand a few key details about the board of directors you are being interviewed for. This can include its mission, vision, and cultural values. If the company has a website, you should visit it periodically before the interview to make sure you are up to date on important information. You could also visit the company's social media pages. Finally, try to do independent research on the company, its CEOs, founders, and executives both on the Internet and through your network. Understanding the company will most certainly give you an edge.

**Know the expected dress code**

This is very important and should never be taken for granted. Never assume you understand what to wear to the interview – make sure you have a clear understanding. You need to fit into the culture of the company at the highest level. The last thing that you want to do is show up for the interview like it's a cocktail party or golf tournament.

**Understand your reason for being there**

Have you ever showed up in an interview looking lost? Do you know how embarrassing this can actually be? This not only reduces your chance of being invited to join as a board member, it can also damage your self-esteem. To avoid this scenario, make sure you properly understand why you are being considered for this position, what the company needs, and how your background fits in.

**Know and articulate your work history, experiences and your value proposition**

Try to list your relevant experiences, expertise, and achievements. Also list roles where you have helped a company grow. You need to clearly and succinctly articulate your value proposition for the company in light of your experiences and expertise. If you can do this very well, it will significantly increase your chances of being selected for the board.

# What should I do during the corporate board of directors interview?

Board of directors interviews can sometimes be very tricky. If you aren't careful enough, you could miss out on getting appointed. There are many expectations for your behavior during a board interview.

**Be confident**

You want to show your interviewers that you have a very vast knowledge about the company and are ready to contribute towards its development as soon as you join. One way to exude confidence is to consistently demonstrate the value proposition that you bring to the board and how it is a match in light of the current board composition and company's direction. Make sure your body language, speech patterns, and behaviors project confidence. As minor as it sounds, fidgeting can limit your chances!

**Provide direct answers**

You don't have all day for an interview. You should always be as direct as possible when answering questions. Observe your answers as you provide them. When it looks like you are staring to digress, stop.

## Respect your interviewers

Take every possible opportunity to leave a lasting impression on your interviewers. The most effective way to do this is to give them the utmost respect. Your interviewers are constantly taking note of both your statements and behavior at every given point in time during the interview, so this can truly make a difference. Be respectful, stay gracious, listen well, comment thoughtfully, and behave appropriately. Even if you seem to have a rapport with the interviewers, do not get so relaxed that you crack excessive jokes or speak too casually.

## Perfect a positive non-verbal attitude

Make sure you maintain comfortable eye contact. Sit properly and maintain good posture. For example, avoid sitting as if you are in a bar or a restaurant. This can convey a professional, poised demeanor. Conduct yourself appropriately, intentionally, and with integrity. Your goal is to demonstrate good judgment in every interaction.

## Be forward and candid

Your answers must be accurate, credible, forward, complete, and honest. No board wants to hire someone who isn't honest or does not project integrity. This requires you to be disciplined, think through your answers, and listen carefully. If it looks like you've made a mistake in details provided, correct it as soon as you can to avoid any suspicion. Practice doing this in a seamless, natural, and credible way.

## Articulate your background, experience, expertise, and ultimate value proposition

Interviews often start with an exchange about your resume as well as your background. You'll need to highlight information about past occupations or any board experiences which prepared you for this role. Other inquiries might be based on past associations and how your connections can influence the company's needs. Also expect questions about your ability to collaborate, understanding of the industry, understanding of the company, its history, and its stakeholders, and understanding of your role as a director.

### Skills and expertise

Expect inquiries about your aptitudes and proficiency issues such as showcasing, finances, communications, advertising, or industry-related information. It is important to focus on high-level experiences and strategy in the relevant industry.

### Connections and networking

Every board member brings new connections to the board and the company. It is not unusual for companies to rely on their board members to open doors, maintain relationships, and be ambassadors. Expect questions about your network and how it can be leveraged to benefit the company.

**Passion and commitment**

Passion and commitment to the company, industry, and stakeholders build a strong case for a solid board applicant. Why do you want to join the board of this specific company? What about its product or people excites you? Are you prepared to stick around long-term through good and bad? Make sure you can genuinely articulate your passion and commitment to the role, company, and industry you are interviewing for.

# What should I look for when I interview for a corporate board position?

A great board's governance practices must include consistently evaluating the work and success of the board overall. Boards must also carefully review potential board members' skills, experiences, and other qualities. It is a good idea to look for the following practices during your interview to identify companies with healthy tendencies and good corporate governance practices:

The board must build up a reported procedure for assessing outer and inward director selections. The nomination board panel is generally responsible for this. They should rally as required to audit and look for qualified candidates whenever there is a board opening. They must also do this when a new director is needed due to a skill review of the board.

The latest assessment of the board, the nomination committee, and any solicitations will influence how potential board members' aptitudes and experiences are evaluated. The board might consider keeping a continuous list of potential board members based on its understanding of the current market.

Boards should evaluate whether they should use a board search consultant. This can guarantee access to a wider selection of applicants. The reported preferred traits of an effective candidate are given to the consultant, who searches out applicants, leads interviews and gives a short list to the designated nominating group.

The panel should create a procedure for interviews and making hiring suggestions. Potential board members' resumes should be circulated. The board can also be meet with nominated candidates.

Nominated and selected directors suitable for casual openings or openings that are due to a board audit must remain up for decision at the following yearly board meeting.

In considering the potential board member's appointment, the nomination panel should respect the continuous progression of the director. Depending on the size and composition of the board and company, potential board members might be welcomed an executive gathering before being formally offered the board position. This allows the potential board member to associate with other executives and perceive how the board functions.

# What should I avoid at the corporate board of directors interview?

Being successful in a board of directors interview requires that you understand what is expected of you at all times. This means that there are dos and don'ts in this process that you must follow. Below are some of the things that you should never do at any board of directors interview.

## Don't be arrogant

Although being confident is good, as it helps your audience sense that you have a good understanding of the subject matter, avoid overdoing it. It may come across as arrogance, which will irritate your interviewers. Don't speak about a subject unless you have been asked to. There are times when it will look like you have made a mistake. As such, you will want to get corrected by your interviewers. If this happens, don't interrupt their flow as your actions could be interpreted as arrogance and disrespect.

## Being scared

This is another issue that can limit your chances of getting appointed. You need to avoid the temptation of expressing yourself in a way which shows that you are scared of your audience. Be in control of the situation by feeling relaxed about providing answers to questions which have been thrown at you. If you have trouble talking to a group of people, then you may need to start working on your speaking skills before attempting a board of directors interview. These will rarely be one-on-one.

## Being sloppy

Even if you think you know the company's culture, do not make assumptions about what you should wear. You want to ensure that you understand what the dress code is for your interview. This can really help to ensure that you aren't taking a shot in the dark. When in doubt, ask! It's better than showing up looking clueless.

## Losing your focus

This is something most people are guilty of. You should not focus more on the benefits attached to the position than on the roles you are expected to play. This can make you leave out little details which will help you get such an appointment. Try as much as you can not to get over excited during the interview and consistently reiterate your value proposition.

## Being clueless about the expectations

Ensure that you understand how you can contribute to the company as a board member. Why did they choose to interview you? What value do you bring in their eyes? This requires researching the role and reviewing your unique fit.

# What should I do after my corporate board of directors interview?

After an interview for a corporate board of directors position, you may not be sure what steps to take next. Below are some ideas of what you can actually do after going through any board of directors interview:

**Analyze your performance**

This is the right time to be honest with yourself about how you actually performed over the course of the interview. One of the ways to get this right is to recall your interviewers' reactions to your answers. Try to remember their body language and responses. It is a good idea to reflect about what you did well and what you can improve.

**Be expectant**

Have you just finished an interview where you think that you performed excellently? This isn't the time to rest on your laurels and keep your fingers crossed. Rather, you should take the opportunity to start practicing the roles you're be expected to fulfill if you are appointed.

Some of what you can do to show that you are optimistic about getting such an appointment are: Always check your mail and expect your phone to ring. This can show that you are optimistic about the board position. You can also ask your interviewers how they will follow up with you. If the interview went well, they will be glad to let you know.

**Thank your interviewers**

This could be the difference between you getting appointed and being turned down. You need to ensure that you have thanked your interviewers before leaving. This has nothing to do with whether you answered questions professionally. Saying thank you shows that you are a true professional – someone they can trust with the highest of responsibility.

**Stay calm**

Over 50% of interviewers are usually interested in the ways people behave before, during, and after an interview. Most of them aren't very interested in the questions they are asking – they are more interested in carefully observing your reactions and how you craft your answers. You must keep your cool, regardless of how you answered the questions thrown at you. This is one period where you don't want to get too emotional. This can limit your chances of being appointed as a member of the board. Just try as much as you can to ensure that you don't fall for this.

# Conclusion

Congratulations! You have just taken a huge step in your board service journey. By reading this book (and completing the worksheets in the appendices) you have invested in your future as a board member.

So what now?

I tried my best to put as much information as possible in this book, but it's still essentially a beginner's guide. And, of course, everyone's board journey is unique, just as every person is unique. Appendix C has a list of organizations that can assist you in taking next steps or share other resources.

If you have any further questions that you would like me to answer in future editions, you can get in touch with me on my website: http://olgamack.com/contact/. Please share your board-related documents, tips, templates, and examples to be used as examples in future editions.

I wish you the best of luck on your journey to board service!

# Appendix A

## Board Readiness Worksheets

These board readiness worksheets can help guide you through the process of getting ready for board service. The Identify Your Target Board Opportunity worksheet can help you consider the type of board, industry, and company you should target based on your past experiences and the value you bring. The Networking Plan can help you identify and categorize key people you should network with, as well as groups to connect with and events to attend. The Board-Ready Thought Leader worksheet will help you plan three stages of board readiness: joining, shaping, and driving the conversation in your relevant industry.

# IDENTIFY YOUR TARGET BOARD OPPORTUNITY

| GOAL | SELF-ASSESSMENT |
|---|---|
| Why do you want to serve on a board? What motivates you? | |
| What kind of experiences have you had? What kind of experiences did you like? Why? Private? Public? Advisory? Startup? F500? Non-profit? | |

| | |
|---|---|
| What industry do you know and like? Why?<br><br>What are your experiences in this industry? Why are they valuable and to whom?<br><br>What related industry do you know and like? Why? | |
| What company size do you know and like? Why?<br><br>What are your alternatives? | |

# NETWORKING PLAN

| DECISION MAKERS | |
| --- | --- |
| BOARD OF DIRECTORS CHAIRPERSON | OTHER MEMBERS OF THE BOARD |
| | |
| CONNECTORS, MENTORS, AND ADVOCATES | |
| INDUSTRY LEADERS/INFLUENCERS (LAWYERS, ACCOUNTANTS, PROFESSIONALS) | EXECUTIVES (CEOs, CFOs, GCs, COOs, VCs, ETC.) |
| | |

| OTHERS | |
|---|---|
| GROUPS &<br>ORGANIZATIONS | EVENTS &<br>CONFERENCES |
| | |

*The following articles was first published on the Association of Corporate Counsel (ACC) Docket (available at http://www.accdocket.com/articles/raising-your-profile-to-get-board-ready.cfm). It explains the Become a Board-Ready Thought Leader worksheet that follows it.*

SC Moatti has the soft smile and all-knowing gaze of a woman who has been there and done it all. We meet at The Battery in San Francisco, where she meets with people twice a week to discuss topics of mutual interest — and she has many interests. After all, Moatti is a technology visionary, a VC investor, and the bestselling author of Mobilized: An Insider's Guide to the Business and Future of Connected Technology (Berrett-Koehler Publishers; May 2, 2016). She also serves on boards of directors for both public and private companies, including mobile technology giant Opera Software (OPERA:Oslo).

SC MoattiMoatti, who started her career as a product professional before becoming an executive at mobile pioneers like Facebook, Trulia, and Nokia, approached her board search pragmatically. She modeled her strategy on previous business development experiences. Moatti has launched and monetized mobile products that are now used by billions of people and have received prestigious awards, including an Emmy nomination. Likewise, she views herself as a product that needs to appeal to a certain market where perfect fit is of the essence: board appointment committees.

"Being board-ready is a new mindset and most people will need to reinvent and re-package themselves at least to some extent to become board-ready," says Moatti. "Reinventing ourselves as many 17 times or even more throughout our career is an essential professional skill to thrive in the ever-changing social, political, and technological landscape." She adds, "In fact, if a professional fails to do that, she will reach the middle career plateau within two to five years."

Moatti draws inspiration from John T. Chambers, executive chairman and former CEO of Cisco Systems. Chambers, who led Cisco as CEO for 20 years, believes that every company must rethink and reinvent itself every three to six years. "It is only logical that people need to do the same to keep with the same changes," Moatti explains. "That's the only way to stay relevant in any business."

Her plan to transition from the C-suite to the boardroom was simple — become a board-ready thought leader in a field, and then look for others who seek this leadership. So, she proactively asked herself:

"How do you go from being an industry expert to becoming a board-ready thought leader?" Moatti developed a surprisingly simple framework to increase her visibility and raise her profile for board opportunities. The framework consists of three steps that are continuously repeated and refined: join, shape, and drive.

## Join the conversation

"The first step is to join the conversation of a function or industry," Moatti explains. This requires a little more than just doing your job well." She recommends doing some combination of the following: chairing or hosting events, hosting speakers, sharing curated content on social media, blogging, or speaking. "This will most certainly connect you with interesting people that you did not know before," says Moatti.

"When I started on this journey, I decided to curate news or tweet something every day, speak once a month, and write a blog entry once a month," shares Moatti. "I started very small." Of course, this required an effort on top of her already loaded professional schedule. "Every day I was looking for something good to retweet," she says. "And it is surprisingly hard to find high-quality writing that adds to the conversation in the sea of mediocre internet writing. Doing so forced me to read and stay current." Writing was also initially challenging for Moatti. "Writing relatively good, well-researched material takes time. And then there's validating, editing, and placing your work in a respectable publication. All of this requires an effort and is not simple," she explains.

The effort paid off, however, and launched Moatti as a key participant in her industry. Soon enough, she found herself on numerous tech panels and included in new conversations. According to Moatti, the opportunity for expedited learning is the greatest reward of going through this conversation-joining process. "It also improved my research skills, my ability to think critically, and my ability to stay current with the developments in my field and business in general," Moatti adds.

**Shape the conversation**

After a while, Moatti was able to do a little more. She started actively commenting on articles written by industry leaders, moderating discussions, and expressing her opinions on Twitter. "It felt only natural to start actively participating in the conversation that I joined," she explains. "Why else would I join, if not to participate?"

Moatti recommends having content-based discussions in your industry or function and being more proactive in seeking interesting opportunities. "In addition to my existing goals, I actively reached out to event organizers to moderate panels. I also contacted blogs to publish my opinions," Moatti says. She developed her own perspectives and began eagerly sharing them on Twitter, instead of merely retweeting the thoughts of others. This helped her grow and gain prominence as an industry leader.

**Drive the conversation**

Eventually, Moatti and her positions became well known in her industry. "I decided to become best in class in my line of business," she explains. "I realized that I have significant views about product development and that writing articles and opinion pieces didn't provide enough space to express the breadth and depth of my thoughts." Moatti realized she was no longer satisfied with simply participating in the industry conversation. "I wanted to drive my discipline in a certain direction," she says. So, when the opportunity to write a book arose, Moatti eagerly took it.

"Writing a book is a whole different endeavor," says Moatti. "It is complex, time-consuming, and difficult." Moatti wrote the manuscript over the summer and published it a year after she signed a contract with a publisher. "It was my summer project, and I loved it!" she says. "Putting words on paper in long form helped me to refine my thoughts, to take bolder and more substantiated stands."

Moatti also regularly leads keynote addresses at

industry conferences. "Panels are largely reactive," Moatti explains. "When you give a keynote speech, the bar is much, much higher. You need to really capture the attention of your audience and meet its needs; it is a performance. You need to be funny, memorable, relevant, current, and entertaining."

Since joining the board of Opera Software a couple of years ago, there hasn't been a dull moment. The company just wrapped up a major strategic initiative culminating in the sale of a major division (half of the business) to a Chinese consortium. "The transaction required regulatory approval across three continents," says Moatti. "Becoming board-ready is only the beginning of another journey, it never ends!"

Although it has required great effort, Moatti has used the "join, shape, drive" framework to gain new skills, refine her perspectives, and successfully transform from an industry expert to a board-ready thought leader. By increasing her visibility as a valuable industry player, Moatti gained the credibility and opportunities needed to become board-ready. And although she has earned positions on boards for both public and private companies, Moatti refuses to rest on her laurels. Always reinventing herself, she is already focused on continuing the cycle. In three to six years, we can expect to see Moatti back at The Battery, discussing her latest visionary transformation.

Complete the *Become a Board-Ready Thought Leader* worksheet on the next page to create your "join, shape, drive" plan.

| STAGE | YOUR ACTIONS |
|---|---|
| Join the conversation | |
| Shape the conversation | |
| Drive the conversation | |

# Appendix B

## Board Profile & Competency Matrix

A competency matrix gives a rundown of crucial competencies a board needs to do a good job. It can be utilized to understand and create your board profile and hone on your unique value proposition. In other words, filling out the competency matrix can help you assess the value you can bring to a board. This tool can also be used to assess the existing competencies your target company's corporate board, which can help you understand if and where you can fit in.

# BOARD PROFILE & COMPETENCY MATRIX

| GENERAL BOARD MEMBER COMPETENCY MATRIX | SELF-ASSESSMENT |
|---|---|
| **Relevant Professional Experience** | |
| Governance | |
| Business/Management | |
| Legal/Regulatory | |
| Human Resources | |
| Accounting/Financial | |
| Risk Management | |
| Public Relations/Media | |
| Other | |
| Other | |
| **Specialized Knowledge** | |
| Government/Public Policy | |
| Community/Stakeholder Relations | |
| Industry/Sector | |
| Other | |
| Other | |

| Personal Skills | |
|---|---|
| Leadership/Teamwork | |
| Strategic Thinking/Planning | |
| Critical Thinking/Problem Solving | |
| Other | |
| Other | |
| **Other** | |
| | |
| | |
| | |
| | |
| | |

# Appendix C

## Board Search Resources

The following table lists prominent organizations that can assist in your board service journey. They range from advocacy groups to executive search services. While there is no substitute for personal research, education, and networking, these groups can provide further resources.

# BOARD SEARCH RESOURCES

| COMPANY | WEBSITE |
| --- | --- |
| 2020 Women on Boards | https://www.2020wob.com/ |
| Advancing Women Execs | http://inawe.com/ |
| Ascend | http://www.ascendleadership.org/ |
| Athena Alliance | https://athenaalliance.org/ |
| Caldwell Partners | http://www.caldwellpartners.com |
| Catalyst | http://www.catalyst.org/corporate-board-services-allies |
| Chadick Ellig | http://chadickellig.com/expertise/ |
| DirectWomen | http://www.directwomen.org |
| Directors & Boards | https://www.directorsandboards.com/ |

| | |
|---|---|
| DiverseCity onBoard | http://diversecityonboard.ca/ |
| Diverse Director DataSource (CalSTRS and CalPERS) | https://www.calstrs.com/diverse-director-datasource |
| DiversifiedSearch | http://diversifiedsearch.com/ |
| Egon Zehnder | https://www.egonzehnder.com/ |
| Equilar Diversity Network | http://www.equilar.com/diversity |
| Executive Leadership Council (ELC) | https://www.elcinfo.com/ |
| HACR | http://www.hacr.org/ |
| Heidrick & Struggles | http://www.heidrick.com/ |
| KPMG Board Leadership Center | https://boardleadership.kpmg.us/ |
| Latino Corporate Directors Association | http://latinocorporatedirectors.org/ |

| LEAP | http://www.leap.org/ |
|------|----------------------|
| MontaRosa | http://montarosa.com/ |
| Savoy | http://savoynetwork.com/category/business/power-300-most-influential-black-corporate-directors/ |
| SpencerStuart | https://www.spencerstuart.com/ |
| Stanford Women on Boards | https://www.gsb.stanford.edu/alumni/communities/womens-programs/stanford-women-boards-initiative |
| theBoardlist | https://theboardlist.com |
| Thirty Percent Coalition | https://www.30percentcoalition.org/ |
| Topmark Advisors | http://topmarkadvisors.com/ |
| Trewstar | https://www.trewstar.com/ |
| U.S. 30% Club | https://30percentclub.org/ |
| Women Corporate Directors (WCD) Foundation | https://www.womencorporatedirectors.org/ |

| Women in the Boardroom | http://womenintheboardroom.com |
|---|---|
| Women Serve on Boards | www.womenserveonboards.com |

# Appendix D

## Examples of Board Documents

The following are illustrative examples of board resumes and board biographies. When crafting your biographies, it can be helpful to read board biographies from your target board opportunities. These can be found on company websites or board member LinkedIn profiles. These model board resumes and biographies can help you to craft your own unique board documents. Please note that all company names and contact information have been anonymized. Some information has been redacted in brackets to preserve anonymity.

# BOARD PROFILE – JANE DOE

janedoe.com    ☐    linkedin.com/in/jdoe☐

janedoe@gmail.com ☐ (415) 555-5555

## CEO / BOARD DIRECTOR

**Insert Professional Headshot Here**

Public board track ◎◎Financial management

◎CEO experience

Global perspect

Silicon Valley inv

## EXECUTIVE BIO

➢ Technology visionary, entrepreneur and investor.

➢ Founding partner of Sample Capital, a Silicon Valley venture capital firm, and Product Community, a global community of product managers, leaders and founders.

➢ Previously, built products that billions of people use at Social Media Co, Mobile Phone Co and Video Game Co Was named by one of Tech Startup's top executives, "a genius at making mobile products people love."

➢ Serves on public & private boards, including mobile technology giant Mobile Tech Co.

➢ Award-winning bestselling author, who frequently gives keynotes on business and technology, including at Prominent Corporate Board Association. Featured in Daily Bugle, Ivy League Business Review, and on NPR.

➤ Lectures at Elite University Graduate School of Business. Elite University MBA, MS in engineering. Speaks 4 languages.

STRATEGIC ASSETS FOR BOARD CONTRIBUTION

**PUBLIC BOARD TRACK RECORD**

➤ Mobile Tech Co. Board of Directors. Member of Remuneration Committee.

➤ Contributed to successful execution of ambitious corporate strategies, including $X00M+ divesture of global public company's business unit to leading [foreign] consortium, returning 150%+ shareholder value.

➤ Elite University Director Consortium Program and Prominent Director Education Program alumni.

**CEO EXPERIENCE**

➤ Created and managed new business unit with record levels of performance and award-nominated mobile service used by billions of people, at Social Media Co and Mobile Phone Co, as CEO / General Manager / Product Leader.

➤ Founding CEO, Social Mobile Startup (acqui-hired by Social Media Co), Sample Capital and Product Community.

## SILICON VALLEY INVESTOR

- ➢ Invest in /advise leading VC-funded Silicon Valley companies including Mobile Message (mobile messaging, $1Bn+ valuation), BioTech Co (biotech, Mayfield portfolio) and Social Saas Co (social SaaS, acquired by Social Media Inc).
- ➢ Assist major private equity firms in evaluation of mobile companies in the context of early-stage investment due diligence.

## FINANCIAL MANAGEMENT

- ➢ Full P&L accountability as CEO / General Manager of several large companies (up to $1Bn).
- ➢ Strong at creating metrics-driven performance management to achieve financial objectives.
- ➢ Exceptional at understanding the drivers of product and business profitability and sustainability.
- ➢ M&A and reverse-IPO financial due diligence, including at Leading Financial Group Inc.

## GLOBAL PERSPECTIVE

- ➤ Executive experience at global Top 10 consumer brands.
- ➤ Product innovation through US / Europe country rollout.
- ➤ Developed and executed international strategies in mobile.
- ➤ Speak English, Spanish, French and Japanese.

# Juanita Pérez

123 Sesame Street, Everytown, CA 91234

jperez2000@hotmail.com 524-555-5555 (cell)

*Insert Professional Headshot Here*

Juanita Pérez recently served as President / CEO of a $XXXm international manufacturing company and has served on boards and committees of privately held companies and non-profit organizations. She is a certified SEC financial expert with an Elite University MBA. Juanita rose through successive leadership roles in global companies with functional expertise in finance, strategy, marketing and product development. Juanita currently serves on boards, and additionally specializes in executive coaching, interim CEO roles and strategic consulting. Since 1989, Juanita has served on 14 Boards both private and not for profit organizations. Her first role as an independent Director was with Family Co, a $Xb family owned manufacturer of industrial equipment. She also served as a Board member of Everytown Incubator, an incubator for technology start-ups; Moneybanks Equity International, a $XXm private equity portfolio company; and Consumer Product Co, a division of Consumer Goods Company. In her role as President/CEO, Juanita managed multiple boards of distinct business units.

Juanita is currently an Independent Director on the boards of Family Matters, Inc., a family owned distribution and fabrication company and Amazing Products, Inc., a components manufacturer, as well as serving as an Advisor for Strategic Consultants Co, a strategy consulting firm for entrepreneurs. Juanita is a past Board Chair and CEO of NatureLearn, a non-profit dedicated to STEM education based on nature literacy.

Most recently, Ms. Pérez was President and CEO of Dundermiff, a $XXXm division of Dundermiff Inc, a global technology company, manufacturing [products]. As President and CEO, Juanita was responsible for 6 business units with 10 manufacturing locations, 6 sales offices, an R&D facility and corporate offices. Prior to Dundermiff, Ms. Pérez served as the VP/GM for Global Marketing and Product Management of Schrute Co., a $X billion division of BEET.

Prior to joining Schrute Co, Juanita Pérez spent two years with Halpert Industries where she was specifically recruited to the leadership team to help prepare the company for private equity sale or IPO.

When Juanita and her husband, Jim, purchased Printing Co, LLC, she utilized her ability to understand consumer behavior to turn around an unprofitable operation. As a business owner, she recognized the changing consumer demand for [service] and transformed the existing business model from [analog] to digital. Ms. Pérez has also held executive level positions with well-regarded brands such as X, Y, and the Z Company.

Ms. Pérez's career began as an International Economist with the U.S. Treasury Department. She earned an MBA from the Business School at the Elite University. She also holds a Masters in International Relations from the Ultimate University School of International Relations and a Bachelors degree from Supreme University.

Juanita has also been a member of Secret Success Org, an invitation-only membership organization of the world's most successful women business leaders.

# JUANITA PÉREZ

123 Sesame Street, Everytown, CA 912345
jperez2000@hotmail.com

524-555-5555 (cell)

## CAREER SUMMARY

**Senior Executive and Board Member** with broad experience improving business results including profitability, market share, geographic expansion, and brand awareness. Demonstrated success in consumer and industrial products in family owned and privately and publicly held companies. Recognized for understanding market behavior and developing strategic plans to drive and meet demand. Innovative leader focused on developing team members to achieve personal and organizational potential.

## PROFESSIONAL EXPERIENCE

**Family Matters, Everytown,FL.**---------------**2017**
**Board Member, Audit Chair**
**The Housing Foundation, Centerville, CA.**-------**2016**
**CFO**
**Amazing Products, Inc., Sampletown, GA**--------**2015**
**present Board Member**
**NatureLearn, Woodsville, GA** ----------------------**2014**
**present Board Member and Executive Director**

**Dundermiff, Inc., Scranton, PA--------------2011-2013**
**President and CEO**

Responsible for $XXXmof revenue with 10 manufacturing sites, X700 employees, and 6 business units. Dundermiff is a global $Xb international technology group with more than 125 years of experience in the areas of specialty materials and advanced technologies. Core markets are the [list] industries. Most sales are B2B, although some products are consumer brands. There are 6 product based global business units with shared regional services of IT, HR, Finance, Legal and Marketing.

**Schrute Co Division of BEET, Scranton, PA-2007 – 2010**

Vice President / General Manager Global Marketing and Product Management

Managed $X billion division manufacturing and selling products to construction industry through rental channel. With global P&L accountability, maintained functional responsibility for engineering, marketing, and product management.

**HALPERT INDUSTRIES, Centerville, WI 2005 – 2007**

**PRINTING CO, LLC, Electric City, OH---2002 – 2007**

Wholesale and retail film processing and printing with both digital and optical printing.

Owner

X INC., Electric City, OH------------------------------1997 – 2003

Division of [company], developing, manufacturing and marketing [products].

Sr. Vice President - Marketing and Product Development

Y PRODUCTS, Charlotte, N.C.--------------1996 – 1997

*Vice President - Market and Product Planning*

Recruited to improve profitability of recently acquired $X00 million division consisting of five business segments, including the [name] brand.

Z COMPANY, Z-town, Wisconsin1---------------995 – 1996, 1983 – 1991

*Director - Corporate Planning and Development* (1995 – 1996)

Directed corporate-wide financial planning, strategic planning and mergers and acquisitions.

Completed 4 acquisitions totaling $XXX million in revenue in less than 2 years.

Conducted 2-year strategic planning process, across all 4 divisions

Director - Marketing and Planning (1989 – 1991)

Senior marketing executive for $X00

million products marketed through wholesale distribution. Managed 45 employees across market research, product management, and programs and promotions. Developed and introduced over 200 new products with sales over $100 million.

*Senior Product Manager* **(1987 – 1989)**

*Product Manager* **(1985 – 1987)**

*Senior Market Analyst* **(1984 – 1985)**

*Financial Analyst - Corporate Planning* **(1983 – 1984)**

## BOARDS OF DIRECTORS

### Current Boards:

**Family Matters, Inc.** – fabricator and distributor
2017 -present

**NatureLearn** science-based education programs and exhibits 2014 present

**Precise Products, Inc.** – custom manufacturer of components 2015 - present

**Strategic Consultants Co.** – strategic consulting company for entrepreneurs 2010 - present

### Past Boards:

**Everytown Incubator** – incubator for new technologies serving the City of Everytown

**Family, Co.** – Family owned industrial products manufacturer

**Consumer Product Co.** – [consumer product] manufacturer

**Sample Group** – Xth largest American manufacturer of mid-range sample products

**ABC Supply Co.** – manufacturer, importer, and retailer of [products]

## EDUCATION

**The Business School, Elite University** – MBA 198XX

**The Ultimate University**, Masters from School of International Relations 19XX

**Supreme University**, Bachelors in History 19XX

**Jane Wong**

**Phone: (650) 555-5555**

**Email: jwong@supremealumni.org**

Insert Professional
Headshot Here

Jane is currently CEO of XYZ Software. XYZ Software is an enterprise software company that is revolutionizing how businesses run in the cloud. XYZ's [technology]-based software platform dynamically optimizes and automates cloud services based on the most critical business objectives.

Jane has rapidly grown enterprise software and consumer internet businesses on the scale of $25M to $3.5B in annual revenue. She was formerly Vice President and General Manager of Software at LMNOP, where she created a new business and platform for offering enterprise software solutions - DevOps, Cybersecurity, Big Data, and App Development - to SMB, Mid-Market, and Large Enterprise customers. Jane had strategy, P&L, and operational responsibilities, and she was focused on engaging customers and partners through several new digital experiences, digital marketing, and specialized sales models to drive growth in net new customers and revenue.

Prior to LMNOP, Jane held six years of product leadership roles at Yahoo!. Most notably, Jane was Senior Director of Product Management for Hello Search & E-Commerce (Hello Shopping, Travel, Autos, and Homes), where she launched consumer internet innovations that drove X00 million daily visits and $X.5 billion in revenue. Jane was also responsible for a number of initiatives to deliver new consumer experiences, improve monetization in digital advertising, increase Search market share, and promote product selection and sales through partnerships.

Prior to joining Hello in 2007, Jane spent three years at ZIA Global Services as a Senior Consultant in the Supply Chain and Customer Relationship Management practices focused on providing supply chain, order management, customer service, and channel marketing solutions to clients in the high-tech, medical device, travel insurance, and retail industries.

Caroline is a Director of Food Co (NASDAQ: [ ]) and Education Inc (NYSE: [ ]). She serves on the Audit and Nominating and Governance Committees for Food Co, and she is the Chair of the Business Advisory Committee for Education Inc and serves on its Compensation Committee. She is also an advisory board member of Advertising Tech, a late stage VC-backed tech company based in San Francisco. She has been recognized as The Prominent Diversity

Association's Top 50 Most Powerful Women in Technology and Tech Industry Business Journal's 40 Under 40.

Jane received a B.S. in Computer Science and an M.S. in Management Science and Engineering, both from Supreme University. She speaks Mandarin Chinese conversationally and plays USVA 4.5 adult league volleyball.

**Sofia Syed**

Scientific Investment Company, LLC

sofiasyed@scientificinvestment.com

415-555-5555

www.scientificinvestment.com

Sofia Syed is the Managing Director of Scientific Investment Company, LLC.Scientific Investment is a 38 year old investment and advisory firm. Ms. Syed is a biotechnology industry leader and successful visionary thinker with more than 40 years of business experience in the life sciences industry and in venture capital investments. She is known for her wisdom and unifying abilities in her Board of Director work with multiple companies and start up venture enterprises. Her international experience and her grasp of the business of science is a unique perspective. She brings value to the classroom as an Adjunct Professor at the University of Gotham in the Department of Analytics and Technology in the School of Management.

Currently, Ms. Syed serves on the Board of Directors of BioTech Leading Co. She serves on the Audit Committee, Nominating and Governance Committee and is Chair of the Compensation Committee. She is a Board member of BioSciences Leaders Inc. She is a Board member of the startup Medical Startup in Metropolis. She also serves on the Board of Advisors to Female Entrepreneurs Org, a non-profit organization dedicated to advancing women entrepreneurs. She serves as Chair of the American [Disease] Association Leadership Board for Silicon Valley. She is a graduate of the Supreme Law School Board of Directors College course, and a member of the Corporate Directors Group which provides continuing education for directors.

From 2000 to 2005, she was a Venture Partner with MGS Capital GmbH, one of the first and largest venture capital firms in Germany. She sourced and invested in three companies and built out their San Francisco office while participating in the raising of their 5th fund of X31 million Euros.

She was a co-founder and CEO of DNA, Inc., a [biotech] company, and wrote the first business plans for [project], as a consultant to Consultant Firm, and for [project], with Dr. Jane Doe, the founder. She was the first biotech analyst on Wall Street for Financial Firm and Banking Giant. She was the creator of two important conferences, The BioTech Conference in Metropolis and The Bio-Pharma-Conference in Europe. She and Katherine Doe started the publication [title], which became the first on line newsletter about biotechnology.

In 2003, she was included in [cultural organization] magazine's annual "Business 100" and received the Alumni Achievement Award from Mega College at Giant University in 2004. Ms. Syed is an avid horseback rider, and mother of a daughter and a step-daughter.

Sofia Syed

123 Sesame Street

Sesame, CA 91234

650 555 5555 mobile 415 555 5555

Email: sofiasyed@scientificinvestment.com

As a Professional Board Member I set clearly defined goals for management filtered by risk assessment and then act as a unifier on the Board for other members to hold management accountable. This makes for a well organized and professional approach to Board meetings. As an independent on the Board I bring broad industry knowledge of Wall Street, Biotechnology trends and strategic thinking.

My work on audit and compensation committees involves acting as Chair, setting agendas and meetings, being the go to person on Say on Pay. I keep a file of data on similar company CEO, CFO and Board pay which helps at annual salary review meetings. I am listed in [website] Capital Registry of Corporate Directors and keep up my education via webinars and seminars. I have attended the Supreme University Board College and meet regularly with the local NACD chapter.

Biotech Leading Co, ([stock symbol]) 2004-Present. Chairman of the Board, elected Chair in 2009, active since 2004 and serve on the Audit Committee and Chair of the Compensation Committee and

Governance and Nomination Committee. Biotech Leading Co. focuses on the development of [type] drugs for major unmet medical needs that treat [type] disorders.

BioSciences Leaders Inc. ([stock symbol]) 2006- Present .Board of Directors, Serve on the Audit, and Chair of the Compensation Committee and the Nomination and Governance Committee. BioSciences Leaders Inc. is engaged in research, development and commercialization of drug delivery systems and antigen based vaccines for [cause].

Chair Emeritus of Metropolis Bio Institute, a nonprofit organization which facilitates education, outreach and work force development in Biotechnology for the Metropolis Area, I focused on diagnostic companies in the Metropolis in genomics. Served as Chair for 5 years.

Board of Advisor to Female Entrepreneurs Org, a nonprofit organization dedicated to supporting women entrepreneurs to achieve financing for high growth ventures.

Board of Advisors, Annual Conference held yearly by Tech Group to facilitate financing of Biotech companies and partnering.

Amercian [Disease] Association Silicon Valley Chapter Board of Directors Work History

MGS Capital, Venture Partner 2000-2004

Venture Partner and Senior Advisor to a one billion Euro European/US venture capital firm. Hired and open the San Francisco office in July 2000. Generated large deal flow through industry contacts, conference speaking and networking. Supervised and conducted research and due diligence on potential investment opportunities. Sourced office space and oversaw construction of 4500 sq feet office. Hired support staff and coordinated deal flow with the Boston and Munich offices. Sourced three local investments: X, Inc., Y Inc. and Z Corp for a total investment of $10 million. Was part of the team raising the fifth fund of X91 Euros in 2001, maintain a 2% carry in that fund. Sat on the Board of Directors of E-Biotech Corporation.

Scientific Investment Company LLC 1998 on going

Managing Member

Managed and raised venture capital partnerships to invest in medical, diagnostic, and biotechnology deals. Fund I started in 1998 to invest in a German based fund, MGS Medical Ventures, a $X3 million Euro fund which invests in early stage life science deals in the US and Europe.

Fund II was started in 2001 and invested in Series A round of XYZ, Inc a Pasadena, CA company with proprietary technology in the [field]. Investments were also made in ABC Pharmaceuticals, Genetics Co and BioTech Gen Inc.

Scientific Investment Company LLC started in 2008 to invest in the public markets in blue chip companies in Vietnam.

DNA, Inc. 1992-1998

Founding CEO-President and Member of the Board of Directors

An early leader in industrial genomics, using [technology] instruments to analyze SNP gene fragments. Company has uncovered [discovery] which it is developing and out licensing for development into [type] drugs. Company is currently focused on pre-natal screening. I secured the initial funding, both debt and equity, and follow-on capital of $X million. Created the initial scientific and Board teams and actively brought the company to San Diego and supported the growth through the IPO.

Scientific Investment Company, Inc. Founder and CEO 1983-1993

Created one of the first investment advisory companies in biotechnology. Created industry newsletter ([title]), conferences (The BioTech Conference in Metropolis and The Bio-Pharma Conference in Europe), Wall Street analyst Financial Firm and Banking Giant, wrote industry and company reports, and did venture capital due diligence and initial company formation. With Consultant Firm wrote the first plan for [project] and [project]. Also reviewed numerous investments and participated in the early round as an investor. Investments included X, Y, and Z. Secured the Z IPO for Banking Giant. Wrote initial plan for [project] with Dr. Jane Doe and participated in the first round of financing. Invested in Metropolis Investment Management, Center Cityl Fund and Major Venture Partners.

Mega Corporation (now owned by Mega AG) 1976-1983

Vice President, Biotechnology Division

Western Regional Sales Manager

National Account Manager: National Institutes of Health

Application Specialist, Medical Products Division, and Life Science Division

Advanced BioTech Company (Division of BioTech Giant) 1975-1976

Medical Diagnostic Sales Representative

Education

State University, Collegeville, Florida

Ph.D. Work in molecular biology

Presidential University Washington, DC

Masters degree in Biological Sciences

MegaCollege, Metropolis, New York

Bachelor of Science in Biology and Chemistry with additional Medical Technologist certification

# Imani Freeman

## CEO, Board Member, Thought Leader

---

*"In today's marketplace, companies must become digital businesses to effectively capitalize on market opportunity or risk extinction. Consequently, regardless of size or industry, the leaders of tomorrow are transforming their companies into software companies today."*

– Imani Freeman, Industry Insights Report 2016

Imani Freeman empowers companies to envision their future and ensure continued relevance in an ever-changing, technology-driven world. For over 25 years, Imani has advised leaders across the globe on scaling and diversifying their businesses throughout the Americas, Europe, and Asia. She has broad industry experience working with F1000 companies in retail, consumer products, utilities, professional services, and technology, with deep expertise in software. Imani is a thought leader in cloud solutions, big data analytics, and business digitization and specializes in helping companies innovate with these technologies while mitigating their associated security and data risks. Imani's ability to ask the right questions and help leaders transform and scale their businesses with technology makes Imani a powerful leader and C-level advisor.

Imani currently serves as CEO at Drone Co, the leading enterprise drone analytics company delivering meaningful business impact to F500 companies by digitally transforming today's work with drones. In this role she divides her time between driving the company's growth strategy and scaling the company's operations globally. Prior to this she was Chief Information Officer at Analytic Insight Inc, a 100% cloud-based software analytics company that delivers actionable insights from the software that runs your business. In her CIO role, Imani wrote a new kind of CIO playbook, enabling cross-company innovation and distributed technology empowerment that enhances stakeholder experience without sacrificing security or compliance.

Before her appointment as CIO, Imani served as SVP of Operations at Analytic Insight Inc. where she led key growth initiatives strengthening the company's move into enterprise and increasing cross company alignment. Imani also was a key player supporting the company's successful IPO and early years as a public company. Prior to this, Imani held multiple leadership positions at ABCSoftware, scaling the company from $2B to $6B. During her time at ABCSoftware, Imani drove over $55 million of annual innovation investments, supporting more than 8 acquisitions for the company and several divestitures. As a lead partner in the development of ABCSoftware's hybrid cloud business, Imani guided the company's transition into a blended business model that supports both on-premise software and cloud-based solution offerings. Imani began her career as a software engineer at Software Consulting Co, where she held many leadership roles during her 17 years. These included running the internal corporate development team for the company's $4B Communications, Media, and Technology business unit, leading the company's $40M global sales operations community of practice, and co-authoring Software Consulting Co's definitive blueprint for go-to-market transformation.

Imani currently serves on the Board of Directors for Digital Growth Co ([stock symbol]), where she is advising the company's digital transformation and go-to-market expansion and is a member of the Audit committee. Imani also serves on the Landmark College Board of Trustees and the [Women's Advocacy Group] Board of Directors.

Imani holds a BA in economics from UC Metropolis and an MBA in strategy and operations from the university's Alpha School of Business. Her market impact recently earned her recognition as a Woman of Influence in Silicon Valley; [Board Publication] Top 20, and as a [Financial Newspaper] Woman of Note. Imani thrives when working with other talented individuals who share her commitment to delivering impact. She is an avid traveler and uses her experiences abroad to deepen her understanding of human interaction and experience.

**Imani Freeman: Helping Companies Scale & Maintain Leadership in the Digital Era**

*"For boards of high-tech ventures looking to add a market-oriented executive with a wealth of positioning and strategy experience, Kelly Kapoor has spent her career giving penetrating advice to C-suite executives on almost every imaginable scenario." -- [Name of Recognizable Industry Expert]*

**Kelly Kapoor** is a tech industry branding/communications expert, and top-level executive advisor/confidante with 30+ years of experience. Her leadership helps companies clarify their vision and accompanying business strategy, establish their brand relevance, and bring their value propositions to market. Kelly's unique ability to reframe a go-to-market approach has helped hundreds of tech companies resolve the issues they face with their marketability, find a clear differentiated path, and achieve global market leadership. She is recognized as a thought leader in communications and in tech influencer circles on the impact of tech and branding on each other.

Kelly's career includes Kapoor Group, the iconic U.S. tech communications agency which she founded in Silicon Valley at age 28 and ran as President and CEO for 25 years. She sold Kapoor Group to Howard Partners in 2015, where she now serves as Managing Partner, Global Technology Practice. During her career, Kapoor directly counselled over 400 technology CEOs and C-level teams on their business and marketing strategies across all phases of growth from start-up to unicorn, to those over several billion in global revenue. When not counselling clients, Kapoor ran all aspects of her firm, through several tech bubbles and a recession or two.

Kelly's expertise includes category creation, brand transformation, crisis counsel, go-to-market strategies, launches, vertical expansion, positioning, thought leadership, executive media-readiness, IPO/M&A navigation, and all aspects of digital communications. Her technology expertise spans multiple sectors: enterprise/cloud, data science, cybersecurity, HR, venture capital, adtech, CRM, supply chain, and consumer ecommerce. Category creation includes ERP with the launch and hypergrowth of Software Co from 1991-1998, CRM with the launch and expansion of Platform Inc from 1992-1999, OLAP with Acme Software, AdTech with the positioning and successful exits of Acme Media, Alpha Ads, ABC Project, XYZ Inc, AcmeLogic, and others within SaaS and cybersecurity.

Kapoor was directly involved in over 10 highly successful tech IPOs, notably, Software Co, Platform Inc, Acme Inc, Commercial Leaders, Service Co, and ABC Project including their positioning to the media/public markets, continued brand relevance, and crisis work. Acquisition work including strategic messaging, brand awareness, and market acceptance for 20 acquisitions, notably, ABC Software, XYZ Computing Inc, Platform Inc, Acme Media, Alpha Ads, and AcmeLogic. Recent brand transformation and crisis counsel includes work with XYZ Media,

Sample Corp., Startup Inc, Entrepreneur Co, 123 Corp and others.

Kapoor is currently on 6 for-profit advisory boards: [list]. Community work includes Metropolis University Advisory Board, and 6 years as President, Board of Trustees, [Religious Organization].

Kapoor received a B.A. in American Studies from Metropolis Colleges, Metropolis, NY in 1984 and her M.S. in Public Relations magna cum laude from Metropolis University in 1985. She has two daughters, Padma, 18, and Parvati, 15, and two very large German Shepherds.

# JOAN F. DOESTEIN

(650) 555-5555

Silicon City, CA

joan@joandoestein.com

## CAREER SUMMARY - QUALIFIED FINANCIAL EXPERT

Joan Doestein is an accomplished Chief Financial Officer and Board Director, with public and private company experience in the technology, financial services, and life sciences industries. She is a qualified financial expert, and has expertise in mergers and acquisitions, scaling business operations, and international expansion. Ms. Doestein has held leadership roles with companies that have shaped the course of the technology industry, such as LMNOP, Memory Block Technology, and X Networking Co, as well as emerging companies. During her career, Ms. Doestein has completed more than $X.5 billion in financings, and $X.5 billion in M&A transactions.

## BOARD OF DIRECTOR - AUDIT CHAIR EXPERT

**GLOBAL FINANCE CO, ([stock symbol]),** a publicly traded company that offers leasing and finance services to a worldwide customer base of [niche industry] and other commercial customers. *Independent Board Director,* 2017– Present. *Audit*

*Committee Member,* 2017 – Present.

**PHARMACY PARTNERSHIP CO,** a private subsidiary of Pharmacy Co that develops pharmaceutical products for women's health. *Independent Board Director,* 2015 – 2017. *Special Committee Chair & Compensation Committee Chair,* 2016 – 2017. Served on special and compensation committees.

**SILICON CITY CREDIT UNION,** a full services credit union with $2 billion in assets. *Supervisory (Audit) Committee Member,* 2013 – 2016.

**FAMILY HOUSE AT SUPREME UNIVERSITY,** provides support and accommodations for the families of children receiving care at Supreme University Children's Hospital. *Audit Committee Member,* 2008 – Present.

**PROFESSIONAL EXPERIENCE**

**XYZ GROUP LLC,** *President*     2010 –  Present

Created a management consulting business providing CFO and Strategic Advisory services for CEOs and Boards of public, and private companies. Clients engage our services to focus their company's strategy for growth, and improve financial and operational performance.

Representative clients, include public companies such as Circuitry Co ([stock symbol]), private equity companies in the [Name] Partner's portfolio, and privately owned companies.

**X NETWORKING CO, ([stock symbol])** 2007 – 2009
*Chief Financial Officer and Senior Vice President*

X Networking Co is a recognized network solutions company, with $X00+ million in revenue. Led the finance, investor relations, audit, information technology, and order admin functions. Hired to turnaround the company's negative trend in financial operating results.

- Turned-around the financial performance of the company. Increased pro-forma net income from an annual loss of ($0.04) per share to a profit of $0.09 - $0.12 per share, in collaboration with the executive team.
- Increased the gross profit margin 250+ basis points. Executed major initiatives, including shifted resources to lower-cost geographies, prioritized product portfolio investments, and spearheaded cross-functional productivity programs.
- Hired a new Finance and IT leadership team. Recruited over 50% of the organization's

professional staff to upgrade technical skill levels and build business partnerships.

**MEMORY BLOCK TECHNOLOGY, ([stock symbol])** 2004 – 2006
*Vice-President Corporate Finance, Treasurer, and Principal Accounting Officer*

Memory Block is a leader in data storage industry, with $X billion in revenue. Led the corporate controllership, FP&A, treasury, and sales & marketing business finance functions.

- Led the financial due diligence and integration for the $2 billion acquisition of MegaTech Corporation.
- Completed a $1.5 billion corporate bond offering and $2.5 billion share repurchase, to offset the share price dilution from the MegaTechr acquisition.
- Built a global financial shared services center, which improved quality and reduced expenses 30%.
- Established both the initial SOX compliance process, and enterprise risk management process.

**DOESTEIN GROUP,** *Independent Consultant* 2001 – 2003

Created a management consulting business, engaged

with clients and delivered services, including: business strategy, business development, and interim executive management.

**INTERNET INFRASTRUCTURE CORPORATION, ([stock symbol])** 2000 2000
*Vice-President and General Manager of the Search Division*

Internet Infrastructure was a hyper-growth internet infrastructure company. Hired to lead the newly formed Search Division with P&L and strategic responsibility for $75 million in revenues.

- Increased business unit revenues 118% from $34 to $75 million, through organic growth and acquisition.

- Successfully completed the $340 million acquisition of Ultimate Corporation, a subsidiary of the Mega Media Company.

**LMNOP COMPANY, ([stock symbol])** 1976 – 2000

LMNOP is a technology industry leader in the imaging, computing, and instrumentation markets. The company grew from $2 to $42 billion in revenue, over this period.

*General Manager*, for an emerging software business, 1998 – 2000

- Built and sold an emerging communications software business for 40X the prior year's revenues.

*Head of Information Technology,* for the Test & Measurement business, 1992 - 1998 Promoted to head the Information Technology function for the $4 billion business. Led the 500+ person organization, located in 12 locations worldwide.

- Led the strategic planning and operational programs to develop the next-generation IT architecture, for the networked enterprise.

- Reduced operational costs ~50%, and re-invested the savings into process-reengineering programs and new business applications.

*Division Controller,* for communications test and network test businesses, 1989 – 1992 Promoted through 5 financial positions (1976 – 1985), to Division Controller of the Printed Circuit Manufacturing Operation (1985 – 1992), to lead the Finance & IT functions for multiple product divisions.

- Collaborated with executive teams to develop strategies for growth, prioritize investments for new product development, and streamlined core business processes and systems.

## EDUCATION

**MASTERS IN BUSINESS ADMINISTRATION,** Silicon City University, 1985

**BACHELORS OF SCIENCE,** Business Admin, Center State University, Central City, 1976

## COMMUNITY AND PROFESSIONAL AFFILIATIONS

**PROMINENT CORPORATE BOARD ASSOCIATION,** Member, 2006 – Present; *Cybersecurity Special Interest Group*, 2017 - Present

**WOMEN'S CORPORATE GROUP,** 2017 – Present

**GLOBAL ASSOCIATION OF FINANCIAL EXECUTIVES,** Member 2004 – Present, *Silicon Valley Chapter Board*, 2014- 2015. Served on the membership committee and academic committee.

**WOMEN FOUNDERS ADVOCACY ANGELS,** Investor, 2016 - Present

**CORPORATE GROWTH GROUP,** Member 2010 – 2013. *Co-Chair Membership Committee*, 2010 – 2011.

# Appendix E

## Board Biography Template

Use this worksheet to build a first draft of your own board biography. Of course, some sections may need to be modified or removed to fit your purposes. And you may choose to add sections as needed. Your career, skills, experiences, and expertise are unique, and your board biography will be as well. Once you have this worksheet completed, feel free to format and edit as you wish. As you can see from Appendix D, there is no one "right" way for a board biography to look. Overall, focus on conveying your unique value as a potential board member.

# BIOGRAPHY FOR

# [INSERT NAME]

[INSERT NAME] has over [#] years of [**INSERT EXPERIENCE e.g., executive management experience**] and an excellent track record in [**INSERT INDUSTRY e.g., consumer electronics**]. These include [public companies, startups, rapid growth, turnaround, consolidation, Internet, mobile, regulated, and traditional businesses]. Her background includes serving as a [**INSERT TITLE e.g., CEO, President, CFO, and COO**], public and private company board member, and a proven top operating executive in businesses ranging from $[#] million to billions in revenue. [**INSERT NAME**] has a reputation as a [**INSERT REPUTATION e.g., talented leader, industry thought leader**]. She strives to **INSERT GOALS e.g.,** create a work environment where open communication, mindful strategy, coordinated execution. [**INSERT NAME**] especially excels at [**INSERT e.g., team-building**]. She has always been active in her community and is a member of many philanthropic groups.

**WORK EXPERIENCE**

- [**Insert Company**], ownership type, revenues, description of business, role, dates of service, and special projects.

- **[Example]**, an early stage startup that has raised $[#] in capital, which is the leading CRM for the biotech industry. General Counsel from 2010 to present. Built legal, HR, and communications teams and processes. Chairman of [**Special Committee or Group**].
- **[Example]**, a leading computer software company which is pioneering the Internet of Things. Legal Counsel from 2006 to 2010. Spearheaded international licensing efforts for [#] product families.

## BOARD EXPERIENCE

- **[Insert Institution/Organization]**, description of organization, cause/beneficiaries, industry, role, dates or service, and special projects.
- **[Nonprofit Example]**, a community advocacy group focused on STEM education through environmental education. Board member from 2012 to present. Co-Chair of Annual Fundraising Gala.
- **[Advisory Board Example]**, a family owned, late stage private company which is a leading [**product**] manufacturer. Advise the family team in the areas of organizational and management development, business process and scaling, strategy, and mentoring. Executive Advisor from 2009 to 2012.

*[Insert paragraph(s) outlining industry circumstances, explaining your career choices. Focus on explaining transition from position to position. Highlight skills gained from experiences and how you have used them in subsequent experiences. Also highlight quantifiable responsibilities (e.g. revenue, number of employees, number of offices, products, regulatory challenges, etc.)]*

*[Insert paragraph highlighting specific examples of strategic, operational, and/or financial expertise. This is where you will emphasize the value you can bring to a board.]*

EDUCATION

[INSERT NAME] earned a BA in [**Major and any honors**] from [**University name**]. She has earned a [**higher degree name**] from [**University name**]. She has also earned the [**list certificates such as CIPP/US**].

CONTACT INFORMATION

[INSERT NAME]

Home Address

Email

Cell

Personal Website

LinkedIn Profile

# About the Author

**Olga V. Mack** is a powerhouse: she's a corporate governance guru, startup advisor, nationally-recognized author, public

speaker, award-winning general counsel, women's advocate, and entrepreneur. Olga earned both her B.A. and J.D. from UC Berkeley. She has received Watermark Make Your Mark, Corporate Counsel of the Year, Women Leaders in Technology Law, and numerous other awards. Olga is also very involved in her community and serves on numerous boards and advisory boards. She is also a passionate women's advocate. She founded the Women Serve on Boards movement (**womenserveonboards.com**) to achieve gender parity on Fortune 500 corporate boards in her lifetime.

Made in the USA
San Bernardino, CA
15 April 2018